THE DESIGNER SCAM

THE DESIGNER SCAM

Colin McDowell

HUTCHINSON
London

© Colin McDowell 1994

The right of Colin McDowell to be identified as Author of this work has
been asserted by Colin McDowell in accordance with the Copyright,
Designs and Patents Act, 1988

ISBN 0 09 1776120

This edition first published in 1994 by
Hutchinson

Random House (UK) Ltd
20 Vauxhall Bridge Road, London SW1V 2SA

Random House Australia (Pty) Ltd
20 Alfred Street, Milsons Point, Sydney, NSW 2061, Australia

Random House New Zealand Ltd
18 Poland Road, Glenfield, Auckland 10, New Zealand

Random House South Africa (Pty) Ltd
PO Box 337, Bergvlei, 2012, South Africa

A CIP catalogue record for this book is available from the British
Library

1 3 5 7 9 8 6 4 2

Typeset by Deltatype Ltd, Ellesmere Port, Wirral
Printed and bound in Great Britain by Clays Ltd, St Ives plc

For Timothy Cooke

Contents

1

Trick or Treat

Has fashion failed? Or have we failed fashion? Although we all require clothes, by no means all of us are convinced that they need be fashionable. We have to be persuaded that fashionable clothes are better – and better for us – than non-fashionable clothes. This is the challenge at the heart of the worldwide fashion industry – the challenge that has given rise to the designer scam; the challenge that sets out to alter our buying habits so radically that we believe that luxuries are, in fact, necessities. For example, on the simplest level, we must be persuaded to be irrational and pay between £50 and £65 for a polo shirt from Ralph Lauren when we can buy a perfectly adequate and remarkably similar one from Marks & Spencer for between £11 and £18. The fact that so many people *are* convinced and *do* buy the expensive item is proof of the enormous success that has attended the designer scam over the last ten years.

It is no surprise that this is a scam that came to dominance in the 1980s – one of the least secure and most volatile decades of the century, when standards, attitudes and expectations received shocks that changed them for ever. Central to the maelstrom of changing approaches to our individuality and to society in general was the rise of fashion as a crucial element in personal happiness and fulfilment. What had for centuries been the preserve of the rich and privileged, what had been kept as exclusive and unattainable by a closed coterie, was suddenly up for grabs. Anyone could join the club of those who considered themselves superior simply because they could afford fashionable clothing. The Millwall Firm wanted to look pristine in Armani? Fine, provided they had the money. A mediocre actor in a second-rate soap wished to wear Versace? The samples were sent immediately. Once you had the label, you were in.

But, as with the Ralph Lauren polo shirt, being 'in' was not enough. You had to be seen to be in. The myth of the superiority of breeding and class has always shown itself in subtle ways that add up to a strong – though whispered – message: we are the Untouchables, the exclusive ones, and by our dress as much as our demeanour shall we be known. But that was a concept too aristocratic for both the Eighties and a scam that relied for its success on numbers. Dwindling pockets of aristocratic old money were not what the fashion industry was after. It wanted the brash, new vulgar money in huge quantities and it knew that the only way to get it was to democratise the old snobberies under the new concept of the designer. 'I wear the label, therefore I am.'

In the Eighties it shaped all elements of life – not only how we dressed and perceived ourselves, not even the way we perceived others by how they were dressed, but our choice of almost everything from the brand of kettle we boiled to what we read. What is the *Independent* if not the first designer newspaper? We began to think that what defined a person was not so much *his* name, attitudes and background, but the names that labelled everything about him – his clothes, watch, toiletries, form of transport – and the attitudes and background *they* brought to him.

The fashion industry was happy. As the chief beneficiary of the new attitudes it had forged, how could it be anything else? Despite their oft-quoted remarks about 'my woman' or 'the man who wears my clothes', designers do not care who buys what they produce. All that matters to most of them is that enough of us do so to please backers and bankers; fund an organisation frequently as complicated and costly as the government of a small country; and support a personal lifestyle which is often an unreal and unhealthy cocktail of the attitudes and moralities of the courts of Genghis Khan, Louis XIV and Ludwig of Bavaria.

All fashion is clothing although, clearly, not all clothing is fashion. At the heart of the designer scam is the concerted attempt of an industry to make us all believe that we need fashion, rather than clothes, not to cover our nakedness but to clothe our self-esteem.

This was the great conspiracy of the Eighties, the decade when the fashion world at every level made a massive effort to turn us all into shoppers. And not just ordinary shoppers. The plot was more precise than that. We were to be turned into label shoppers. 'Designer' became a catch-all expression used, misused and abused, in order to label anything with pretensions to exclusivity and originality. 'Designer stationery', 'Designer bathroom accessories', 'Designer car interiors' had nothing to do with a specific designer, although many dress designers have put their names to such products. They were generic terms for superiority.

The designer scam worked because it was to do with taste: an imponderable, unquantifiable element. But, because that element had certain old-fashioned and class connotations, a new word was coined. Style was what was sexy, new and 'now'. Hadn't Nancy White, editor of *Harper's Bazaar* in the late Fifties, said, 'the woman of taste is a woman of adventure'? Well, now the adventure was style and everyone could aspire to it – man, woman and child.

What is this scam that cost us all so much money? What does the purchase of a designer object go towards paying? Is a high percentage of it channelled into improving working conditions and increasing the salaries of the people who toil in this most exploitative of industries? Of course not. Our money is used to inflate the standing of the designer, to make an already exotic way of life even more so; it is used to pay for advertising aimed at making us feel inadequate until we have spent even more money buying into a lifestyle peddled by the editorial pages of news-papers and magazines; our money is used to support the disregard for equality that pays poor basic wages, but hands top models $20,000 for a day's work and gives the photographer shooting them double that amount, and expects us to approve and even be excited by such sums; it is used to finance 'bread and circus' fashion shows that can cost well over $150,000 for a brief and irrelevant twenty minutes; it is used for 'freebie' trips, gifts and all the privilege and luxury heaped on the journalists who work in fashion; it is, in brief, used endlessly against us in order to keep designer clothes obscenely overpriced, and to make them appear so desirable, so essential that we continue to pay.

The designer scam sets out to convince us that a certain level of wealth, a certain style of living, a certain assessment of what is important in life raises us above criticism and accountability. To be fashionable, it suggests, is not merely to live on a level of privilege. It is also about being able to do so on the level of Caesar's wife.

The extravagance of the world of high fashion is crumbling. The music falters. The dancers trip. After barely more than a hundred years as a public force, fashion – initiated as a bourgeois pleasure by Charles Frederick Worth in the Second Empire – has failed. Fashion is collapsing as we move into the twenty-first century, and the reason it is doing so is not hard to find. The past decade has been the most destructive in the history of fashion because cynicism and self-seeking were allowed to become the driving force of the industry. No artistic consideration has the power now to overrule the possibility of financial gain. In a world where costs must be kept down – and ruthlessly cut even at the expense of quality – not to improve the product but to increase the margin of profit, the needs of the customer are largely ignored. The industry can carry on with impunity as it knows that the consumers hardly know what quality is, do not care to look for it and put all their faith in the talismanic power of the label.

It was not always thus. In the 1950s Balenciaga refused to allow his name to be put on goods manufactured under licence, his argument being that to do so would not only confuse the customer, but, much more importantly, would destroy the purity of his vision and damage his integrity as a creator. To do so merely in order to make money was for him a preposterous proposal. It is a measure of how low fashion has slipped that such reasoning by a designer today would be taken as proof of madness, or at least, naivety.

Of course, all industries, all endeavours, all artistic enterprises require funding. But what has happened in the fashion world that makes today's designers, their works and attitudes so shoddy compared with Balenciaga's is the fact that money is now the bedrock of the industry. And we allow it to be. That is why fashion is so debased. Few worlds can be relied on to impose their standards without vigilance from outside, and fashion is no exception.

Fashion has failed becaused the public have failed. We don't consider the fashion world important. We are exploited, as all people are exploited, because of ignorance. Fashion, its social significance and economic value apart, is still considered frivolous, of interest only to a privileged, vacuous few. That is why it is still not an academic study in schools, examined at GCSE. The ignorance that such attitudes encourage is the reason why fashion has reached the dangerous point where the practitioners and cognoscenti, like those involved in modern art, avant-garde music and experimental writing, have left the public behind and have done so with pleasure.

The fashion world is deeply insecure. It is ruled by fear. Where everything is opinion and interpretation and little is fact, instability and unease flourish. Like any artist, a dress designer has no set of rules by which to measure his success – nothing more tangible than the opinion of those for whom he works. In the days when dressmaking was an intimate, personal art he received the necessary feedback from his customers. Now he must please press, backers and retailers as well.

Fear makes fashion extravagant, not just in ideas and in prices, but also in the sheer numbers of people involved. It is an overcrowded world. There are too many designers producing far too many ideas for a market which is finite. Too many of these ideas are derivative, but this alone does not mean that they will not succeed. Most of them are conceived to be sterile, were expected to be stillborn and have little purpose other than to fill a catwalk, utilise a certain material or point up a new direction. They are not put into production because they were never designed to be sold and, if they cannot be sold, they have no life expectancy beyond their brief moment in the spotlight of the designer's show. But they help sustain the appearance of unbridled creativity, and, incidentally, of consumer choice (most designer clothing actually varies very little) and they make fashion seem much more volatile and inventive than its true, conservative nature.

The fashion world is prodigal at all levels. Too many students are trained; too many journalists are employed; too many shops and boutiques fight each other for a share of a diminishing market. The lean, clean Nineties have had remarkably little effect in paring down all this excess, even though businesses have folded, boutiques have disappeared and magazines are in serious financial difficulties. The fashion industry is still able to lure people, despite the fact that it is chronically over-subscribed. Their chances of achieving success become slimmer each year but that is no deterrent. Journalists sacked from full-time jobs can make a good living as freelancers; failed designers become stylists and general entrepreneurs in a business which, by its very nature – cyclical, hysterical and insecure – requires go-betweens and fixers at all levels; fashion graduates who find no work in design or journalism go into public relations. Can it go on, or will fashion eventually end up like that other prodigal profession, the theatre, where, regardless of talent, a considerable number of actors, producers and directors expect to spend long periods 'resting'?

Like acting, fashion design is not difficult for someone with a certain level of ability. Reliant as they are on intuition, neither requires intellect or learning. Thousands of people can reach a certain level in either field, and they have their places. 'Bit' parts on TV, supporting roles in rep, designing for mass-market firms or acting as anonymous creative assistants to famous designers – it is amazing how much of the slack can be taken up by those who do not make too many demands on themselves and live in hope. That hope is almost always disappointed – the break, if it comes, normally does so early in a career rather than later. But if you are in love with theatre, nothing else will do. If you are a fashion freak, you will remain one to your dying day.

In fashion the mass of competent talent acts like a comfort blanket to the business because everyone knows there is plenty more where it came from. For the designers, it is not such good news. They know how expendable they are if they do not achieve a profile. Who wants a 46-year-old designer in a profession where youth is at a premium and when a 23-year-old – malleable, fresh and eager – comes at half the price? Only established figures are allowed to grow old in fashion – and even then they are not always safe. Far too many designers have suffered the indignity of falling flat on their face when the financial mat has been tugged from under their feet.

For the individual such treatment is a tragedy, but does it matter for the business? How many dress designers does the world really need? Just how much fashion do we want? For every Yves Saint Laurent or Giorgio Armani, the *crème de la crème* equivalent of the century's great actors such as Sir Laurence Olivier or Sir John Gielgud, there is a plethora of second- or third-rate designers working in Milan, Paris or New York, all of whom have a following and make money, but none of whom actually count.

Any designer who has even a cursory knowledge of the history of the profession must be brought up short by the ghostly roll-call of names once famous, now barely familiar; the names once familiar, now quite unknown. Paris before World War I? Yes, of course, Worth. And? How many designers or even fashion journalists could add more names? And yet *la Grande Couture* was awash with illustrious practitioners at this most productive and exotic time for dress design. Maison Callot, run by three sisters, dictated to the world of fashion for two decades. Mme Cheruit was not only a great couturier, she was one of the personalities of Paris. Doeuillet, who trained at Callot, was one of the most influential dressmakers of the time. No one could have predicted that their names would have sunk so totally into oblivion in less than a hundred years. There were others, slightly less exalted but famed and revered in their time: Beer; Jenny; the milliners Rose Descat and Reboux. Who knows of them now?

Elitist couturiers and milliners – how can their names be expected to survive in a ready-to-wear culture, you might argue. So, how many people today know the name of Edward L. Mayer, who was recognised as America's first and greatest ready-to-wear designer in the decade before World War I? Or that of Bianca Mosca, who was designing in London in the Forties? Or Lucien Lelong, one of the Fifties 'greats', or even Hattie Carnegie, considered by many to be the mother of American fashion, the woman who dominated the New York fashion scene for two decades? Who knows these names now? No one outside the fashion historian's world – and there is no reason why they should. In the era of Poiret, Chanel and Schiaparelli those three are the names that matter –just as that of Rembrandt makes irrelevant ,the other painters in Holland in his time for all but specialists in the history of art.

But it is a salutary exercise to consider which designers from the last twenty years will have a reputation that lasts until the end of the next century. Of only one can we be certain. The name of Yves

Saint Laurent has already become part of twentieth-century history, just as did those of Chanel and Dior before him. All others are problematical. My vote would go to Armani and Ralph Lauren. It seems doubtful that the names of any others will survive in any meaningful sense for more than twenty-five years after their deaths. Designers of the calibre of Versace and Lagerfeld make exciting and sometimes beautiful clothes, but what they achieve can in no sense be seen as a historically lasting statement for their times. For the rest, even though they include some of my personal favourites, only oblivion awaits.

Names are not merely kept alive by clothes. Some of the names from the past that are commonly known today conjure up no picture of clothes at all. Who can say anything about Nina Ricci's fashion? Who could describe the clothes of Jeanne Lanvin? What is remembered of Patou? Their names are known by their perfumes – more durable and less inclined to date than clothes could ever be – rather than their *métier*. There is an interesting irony in a situation where highly creative people are remembered for the creative efforts of others – the men and women who conceived, produced and packaged the scent that bears the couturier's name. Ricci's L'Air du Temps was created in 1948, Lanvin's Arpège in 1927 and Patou's Joy in 1935: who recalls the clothes they designed in those years?

A strong-selling fragrance can keep a couturier's name to the fore long after interest in his clothes has waned. Paco Rabanne is a classic example – as is Pierre Cardin – of a name that has ceased to have any real meaning in current fashion and yet is well known to people for whom the names of better designers are completely unrecognisable. The fortunes of fame are selective as well as volatile. Of the current names likely to be kept alive by their perfumes, the strongest contender is surely Calvin Klein, whose Obsession has all the signs of staying power.

But most designers think of the present more than the future.

Although they would like to feel that they have a place in history, it is their importance *now* that really matters. They know that being good – even very good – at their job is not enough to guarantee the fame that breeds continuity and brings fortune. That is why they must project themselves and their design decisions as forcibly as they can.

Every top designer needs to think that he is a household name. Each one wishes to be wealthy, not necessarily for personal greed, but because in a business where success must be – and can only be – measured commercially, money amassed is the equivalent of a beatific hand laid on the head by the industry's god, who is Mammon. All wish to see their vision made manifest on the streets because it symbolises a power not only over women and the choices they make, but also within the fashion business itself – heady wine for any creator. But what really counts, what really gives a designer that buzz of excitement or warmth of contentment (depending on temperament) is the status they can achieve when, like Valentino in Italy, they become part of the world they dress: the kings of the social scenes that really count.

Valentino is *the* social designer of Italy – a fact that concerns Armani, a greater designer in every sense, not at all. But if Val makes a splash in New York, there is no rest at Casa Versace until their boy has made a bigger one. If Valentino dines with a head of state – and, bizarre as it seems, dressmakers can do this – Versace must dine with another. But, still, where class counts, Valentino remains comfortably ahead. His only rival on the social scene is the New York-based designer Oscar de la Renta who, if he does not actually dine with kings, certainly breaks bread with presidents and travels with the likes of Henry Kissinger, with whom he visited China a few years ago. International society adores them both – a fact that does no harm at all to the business of selling frocks in considerable numbers.

However, the vast majority of clothes one sees on the street, rather than in magazines, the clothes people actually wear, are not those created by the people who spring to mind when the word 'designer' is mentioned. The Frenchman Louis Féraud is a case in point. One of the bestselling fashion houses of the Eighties, Féraud became so not by social jockeying, not by spending huge amounts on advertising, but by looking after the nuts-and-bolts end of the business – pouring money into modern factory equipment, ensuring that clothes were shipped on time, designing to an international level of taste and, above all, insisting on sound retailing practice. Such approaches have brought wealth, if not kudos.

But, for the majority of designers, status is the spur once a certain level has been reached in the fashion consciousness of the world. Status once achieved must be preserved by assuming a personal elusiveness that keeps alive the illusion of godlike grandeur which most of the world's top designers seem to require for their peace of mind. And it is at that point that a kind of madness creeps in. Most of the world's great designers live on a level of paranoia, obsessive secrecy and distrust of all but their personal staff that makes any real contact with those outside their world as unlikely as the Queen of England making friends in a supermarket queue.

The Emperor's New Clothes syndrome especially haunts fashion designers – at each collection they quiver in case someone will say that their clothes are wrong for the time, lack taste, are unflattering to women and, greatest of all fears, unwearable. Unwearable equals unsaleable. For all the talk of high artistic endeavour, interpretation of the Zeitgeist and the creation of beauty, the business of dress design is just that: business. The only good dress, as rag-trade cynics well know, is the bought dress. If it stays on the hanger it has failed. Such a failure does not mean that a designer is doomed – the fashion world is generous, and rich enough to allow a little leeway, take up a little slack and go on without too much nervous twittering provided that the designer buckles down, works harder and doesn't have a repeat failure next season. But the bottom line is sales.

It is part of the designer scam that the fashion world is a highly secretive one. Success or failure can only by judged from outside by the carefully contrived public faces that companies present. Balance sheets, investments and profits are jealously guarded from anyone outside the firm. Lies are blatantly told by many designers in order to keep retailers, suppliers, subcontractors and factory managers in a happy state of ignorance for as long as possible.

Perceptive observers who notice the tell-tale signs – lukewarm reception of the show by the press, cutbacks in orders, delays in shipping and so on – are fobbed off with bland assurances when they dare to ask how things are going. 'Marvellously,' a spokesperson replies, ignoring the evidence of the balance sheet he has just been studying. 'We've had a fabulous season. In fact, we're thinking of doing a second line. We are ready for expansion now. We project a very strong upcoming year.' The same person will be saying this up to the very morning when the bombshell is dropped and the firm files for bankruptcy or dismisses its designer in a blaze of publicity, fanned by accusations, denunciations and denials.

It would be easy to say that such performances reflect the deep cynicism of the fashion world, but that is only half the story. They also reflect the naivety and hope that runs through that world. Everybody wants to believe that things will get better and there is the fantasy that if you say something enough times it will come true. The fashion world believes in positive thinking, but it is positive thinking with a flip side. The good part is seen in the sheer dedication of most people who work in a fashion house. Unlike workers in other fields, they all feel so personally involved and so value their contribution to the overall scheme that they work hours that would not even be considered in most industries. Again, like the theatre, fashion works on the premise that the show must go on and, in order that it might, individuals, from the designer down, must become cogs in a complicated series of wheels running a machine much bigger than any of them. When I worked in fashion in Italy, the pattern for at least six weeks before a collection was a ruthless one: seven days per week, 8 am to midnight and beyond, with no breaks and no backsliding. It was exhausting not only because of the length of the working day and week but because everyone was so deeply involved with the business of creativity that it was impossible to pull away in order to recharge body, soul or mind.

The negative side of positive thinking comes from this same intense involvement. A group of people in such an inward-looking situation does not always find it easy to maintain the critical faculty essential in all artistic effort. There is often an element of sycophancy in the great houses of the fashion world. A volatile and often hysterical designer must not have his ego dented by adverse comment. Within the walls of a fashion house all criticism is stilled. It is the cynicism-versus-hope formula again. Cynical manipulators who surround the designer will not permit criticism; the designer himself will almost certainly not respond to it; many of the young assistants are so much in love with his talent that they are raised up on a pink cloud of hope. A dress doesn't look quite right at a fitting? Don't worry. It will! Oh, but it *will*!

Costs are so high, workmanship is at such a premium and time is always so short that, by the time a dress appears for fitting on a house model – its first public viewing since the sketch was agreed and the fabric assigned – it is almost always too late to be critical. It is easier to say that a dress is 'chic' than to begin criticising or even questioning basic design faults in the original concept. A fitting is not usually seen as an opportunity to redesign or alter the original idea in any major way. It is a time for adjustments – repositioning a pocket, narrowing a lapel, modifying the hemline – and these can be achieved within an overall framework of enthusiasm: 'Very chic,' the chorus goes as the house model appears. A pause. 'Have the proportions of the collar been changed?' a tentative voice enquires. The head of the workroom responsible for the garment indignantly refutes this slur. The drawing is produced. Sides are taken. After much discussion it is tacitly agreed that the 'very chic' dress is not so chic that it cannot be improved upon. The repinning begins. At no time in the whole process – which can take a few minutes or over an hour – does anyone say that the dress is badly designed or that someone has got it wrong.

The designer scam works within the industry as well as outside. It ensures that the maestro does not have to stoop to criticism from the lowly ones whom he employs. In every fashion house I have ever visited, adverse comment is always made in whispers, behind trembling hands; even then, if something is wrong, a scapegoat is found so that no blame is laid at the designer's door.

In a world where there is no blame, praise becomes meaningless. This is a dangerous situation for business or artistic endeavours: it strips away internal rigour and lays the way open for unchecked indulgence. The same cotton-wool treatment – far removed from the ruthless laws of the marketplace – extends outside the designer's own house to the PR people and journalists.

God help the journalist who even hints that the maestro has not hit form this season. Designers have frequently reacted hysterically to criticism even from doyennes of fashion journalism such as the *International Herald Tribune*'s Suzy Menkes and Carrie Donovan of the *New York Times*, both of whom, despite their exalted status, have been banned from shows by designers whom in the previous season they panned.

To ban a journalist from a show is the equivalent of a weak school teacher sending a disruptive pupil to stand in the corridor – and just as childish. But it works during the highly stressed period of the collections, and designers feel that it concentrates the mind, encourages *les autres* and ensures that no one else will be so foolish as to criticise them again in the next few seasons.

The designer scam is calculated to make us forget all of this and believe that the world of high fashion is harmonious, rational and ordered. To find the truth we must look at the reality behind the sham.

2

Waves and Watersheds

Christian Lacroix is a sensitive and mild-mannered man. In love with the colours of Provence, an Anglophile and opera-lover, he has many admirable qualities. It is not easy to see him as a villain, but it cannot be denied that his impact on fashion, if not villainous in inspiration, has been pernicious in its effects. Quite simply, his was the dagger that plunged deep into the body of fashion and turned the traditional basis of all fashion design – the couture –from a dignified, gracious, and perhaps rather staid old lady into an all-singing, all-dancing good-time girl game for anything flirty.

To kill couture by making it a laughing stock is not such a great crime. What Lacroix's action exposed was the weakness of traditional fashion attitudes. By destroying the concept of taste – again, not such a terrible crime – he made plain how empty of ideas modern fashion was. When Christian Lacroix showed his first major couture collection for Patou to a delighted audience in 1985 he set fashion on a new path for which it was – and still is – little prepared. It was the only path fashion could take after the idiocy of modern couture had been laid bare. This is the path that will finally kill the hegemony of Paris as the capital of fashion. This path leads downtown to youth, casualness and informality. This path leads directly to the twenty-first century. This path is one that Lacroix could never have dreamed he was opening up on that fateful day.

Lacroix's approach to couture – iconoclastic, jokey, irreverent – was the first powerful proof of the designer scam in the Eighties.

But, to understand its effects, it is necessary to examine the concept of couture.

The Eighties was the decade of linguistic solecism. The most notoriously misused word was 'gay', but 'haute couture' was also stretched to include things not conveyed by the expression in its original and precise form. True *haute couture* was clothing made to the exact measurement of the client and fitted at least three times to ensure perfection. Couture was largely a tailor's art and showed to greatest advantage in the coats, suits and daydresses that formed the backbone of high fashion from the early 1930s to the late 1950s. It was essentially an understated art form that was only fully appreciated by those who had taken the trouble to understand how clothes were actually made. Informed clients such as socialite Mona Bismarck dedicated their lives to their couturier's art. Diana Vreeland, greatest of fashion journalists, told me that when her friend Mona heard that Balenciaga had closed his dressmaking establishment she locked herself into her villa on Capri and did not emerge for three days, so great was her grief. Although much less emotionally extravagant, Mrs Vreeland herself admitted that she found fittings, long and tiring though they were, completely engrossing because they were an endlessly fascinating, learning experience. Her view was that fashion ceased to be of intellectual interest when couture was no longer its driving force.

Couture lost centre stage at the end of the Fifties, not simply because costs had risen so dramatically as to price it out of the market. There are always people able to afford indulgence, no matter what the price. It lost relevance because the attitude of women had changed. Hand-made clothing, often requiring the client to spend as much as three weeks in Paris each season being fitted, choosing accessories and visiting the *corsetière*, simply did not seem worth the effort any more in a world where youthful, casual, informal clothing was taking the stage. A new woman, with radically different attitudes and needs as well as considerable

17

personal spending power, had emerged. Kept-woman, rich-bitch dress conforming to male standards and bankrolled by male earnings was not what she required. She was not interested in understanding the dressmaker's art or appreciating the tailor's skills. She did not want to be informed about clothing; she wanted to be informal.

The respectability of spending developed in the Fifties as wealth began to percolate down to the middle classes and fashion was seen increasingly as a young person's concern. It was self-evident, as manufacturing skills increased and mass-production techniques enabled quality to be kept high while prices were brought down, that the fashion business could grow at any speed and to whatever level was required. The question became not 'At what level can we produce?' but 'At what level will we *sell*?' Buying fashionable clothes, previously a predominantly middle-class pastime, became an occupation for all, especially in the affluent 1960s when, for the first time in history, there was a demand for clothes geared exclusively to the young market.

Nancy White made clear the role of magazines as selling tools. 'The more fashion we can put on the backs of American women,' she said, 'at whatever prices they can afford, the better for all of us.' She was speaking for the whole industry. And it all seemed so easy then. The new markets would keep sales high at all levels. No one saw the flaw. By reducing the age of fashion desirability in their clothes, designers limited their market at the very moment when they could have expanded it.

It is easy for a young woman to dress as if she were older; it is very difficult for an older woman to dress convincingly – or even comfortably – in styles created with a young woman in mind. The great couturiers of the past knew precisely who was the customer for their expensive clothes, hand-made to the measurements of the individual. They were women rarely under 25 and more likely to be nearer 40 than 30. They were rich. They were leisured. They were women for whom elegance was the goal; women whose husbands and lovers – who usually paid the bills – wanted them to look alluring and seductive. They expected their clothes to give them class, even dignity.

Couturiers showed their clothes to these women on models who were an idealised mirror-image of themselves. Old-style models had a sophistication and worldliness which were considered much more important than perfection of figure. In the days when fashion was personal, a fashion show was an intimate occasion. A customer identified with models who, perhaps, did not have the perfect bust or the classic profile and, for that reason, she identified also with the clothes. No couturier put any great stress on height when choosing models. Some did not worry too much about shape – as a Balenciaga *vendeuse* once reassured a customer, 'Oh, monsieur *likes* a certain amount of stomach.'

Women with 'a certain amount of stomach' were the ones who had the money to pay for the couture. They wanted clothes that flattered their age and disguised their imperfections. They did not wish to look gauche and young. The women they admired – Katharine Hepburn, Edwige Feuillière, Marlene Dietrich, Lauren Bacall – were, if not all of a certain age, certainly not schoolgirls. They were confident, experienced and as far removed as possible from the *ingénue*.

Then, in 1956, Brigitte Bardot appeared in *And God Created Woman*, a film which made clear the dramatic change that had taken place in women and their attitudes. Suddenly the desirable woman was the sex kitten and, by definition, she was young. The desirable figure was nubile. The desirable walk was pert. Playful flirtatiousness entered the lexicon of sexuality in a way it had not since the days of Victorian child pornography. Above all, informality became sexy. The sleeveless gingham frock, with artless frills, ousted the draped silk gown with the flying panel. It was chic not to be chic. The individual grew in status the more non-status her dress was.

Informality is the major characteristic of dress in the second half of the twentieth century. Time-honoured social concepts have been swept away on its tide. What nation still preserves the idea of Sunday best? What modern man can fail to laugh at the lifestyle exemplified in Austin Reed's list of 'essentials' published in 1930 in a little booklet entitled *Packing Predicaments*, which included under the heading 'The Absolutely Vitals' a smoking jacket, coloured silk handkerchiefs, suspenders, boot trees, folding coat-hangers and soft and stiff collars to be packed for a trip? Although many men would still have considered them 'vitals' in the 1950s, no one would now. In another fifty years the items will seem as mysterious and incomprehensible as Georgian spatterdashes do today.

Or what of these diktats from Geneviève Antoine Dariaux, directice of the house of Nina Ricci in the Fifties? 'Whether she is entertained in a restaurant or at the home of friends, a woman luncheon guest must always wear a hat.' 'Women should always wear gloves, whenever they go out.' 'A good suit is the essential foundation of an elegant woman's wardrobe.' When we realise how seriously such comments were taken we begin to understand the sheer force of the Bardot bombshell. Elegance was no longer the prerogative and reward of age. Nobody – young or old – wanted it any more in the 1960s, and they have never wanted it since.

Courrèges, Cardin, Mary Quant and all the inventive but now forgotten designers who sprang up in Paris and London to serve a need were only interested in dressing the young. Fashion became egalitarian for the first time in history. Or so it was thought. In fact, it became no such thing. Fashion merely changed its currency. Whereas, in the past, money, dignity and age had mattered, now youth, vitality and informality were what counted on the fashion exchange.

The rebirth of couture – a very different sort of couture – had its promptings in an unlikely source. Ready-to-wear suffered a terrible shock in 1981. That year saw the arrival in Paris of a group of radical Japanese designers, and the waves that spread out from fashion's epicentre rocked the boat in Milan, London and New York. For a while, it looked like Western fashion's Pearl Harbor. Japanese design seemed to strike at the very core of fashion. Rei Kawakubo of Comme des Garçons, Yohji Yamamoto and their compatriots approached dress from such a fundamentally different viewpoint that they could almost have come from another planet. Completely new cuts, totally different standards of workmanship, absolutely new shapes electrified the fashion world and petrified most other designers. After an initial gulp, the fashion press grew enthusiastic, art students throughout the world fell madly in love, and Japanese fashion was hailed as a force.

So it was, but not in the way people thought at the time. If these misaligned clothes were difficult to understand, they were even more difficult to wear with confidence. Clothes that make us insecure or ill at ease – will people laugh? how many of my friends will understand them? who will know simply by looking how much they have cost? – are not easy to sell. Despite the acres of space devoted to photographs – and these clothes *did* photograph very arrestingly – and the miles of type dedicated to explaining them, Japanese fashion's true impact on how women dressed was minimal. Certainly, buyers from the top fashion stores fought over what they considered key looks and seminal lines but they bought in numbers that could be counted on the fingers of one hand, usually with no more commitment than to create talking-point displays in store windows or to lure people into departments reassuringly stocked with fashion they could understand.

What was wrong with Japan's new-wave fashion that took the originality of Kenzo and the purity of Issey Miyake so much further forward? Why did such a strong, new fashion approach fail to change the way women dressed in the Eighties? Why did the last five years of the decade see women wearing 'power' suits, miniskirts and all the regressive panoply of anti-feminist dress when fashion in the first few years of the Eighties had been so strongly feminist-led? Why did the Japanese approach to dress – neo-rationalist, we were told at the time – fail as significantly as the first rational dress movement had a hundred years earlier? Why, above all, did the trade turn its back on what appeared to be the first truly new movement in fashion since the 1920s?

A fashion only becomes *the* fashion if it has a broad-based appeal. Mass market manufacturers must have the confidence that women at large want it and will wear it. Only with this confidence is a fashion taken up, adapted and disseminated in numbers that have any significance. Buyers spend a lot of time questioning. Will it go in Bal Harbor? Can I shift this in any significant numbers in Düsseldorf? Is Glasgow ready? In other words – will this *sell*? Mass-manufacturers question even more. At the root of all their queries is the bedrock one – to how many age groups can this fashion appeal? Fashion writers can turn purple with excitement, stylists and photographers can tantalise with the most marvellous of photographs, but if a line looks wrong in a size 12 it is doomed – let alone in a 14, reputedly the size of Liz Tilberis, the buxom editor of US *Harper's Bazaar*. The problem with Japanese fashion was the same problem of the over-hyped fashion emerging from the London art schools of the time, and both died for the same reason. They were ageist.

Young women adored both. Young women frequently looked marvellous in both. But the magic stopped there – and hard-headed people at the business end of the trade knew that women over 30 would feel disorientated and insecure in such radically new cuts. They did not invest in the neo-rationalism. They looked elsewhere and, unlikely as it sounds, found their answer in the home of Western fashion.

Couture had slept undisturbed for almost twenty years – although it was still shown by designers as a self-indulgence affordable by those with lucrative perfume licences or backed by multinational companies. Nevertheless, the couture shows were considered unimportant in terms of fashion developments and very few major fashion journalists took the time to go and see them. Rightly, they judged them irrelevant to the needs of their readers.

In the late 1970s, the slightest breeze of change began to blow through the perfumed halls of Paris. The petrol princesses, awash with money, wished to spend it on clothes that produced the most dramatic and obvious effects. Designers realised that the only area of couture that could be exploited to service this need for ostentation was evening wear. Rich embroidery in the crudest colours was piled on poorly made dresses to produce shiny effects of stupefying vulgarity. Middle Eastern princesses and their taste were of no interest to the rest of the fashionable world, and for the majority couture still slumbered. The kiss that awakened it was given by Christian Lacroix, who seemed to be fashion's Prince Charming but who has subsequently appeared to be nearer its Jack the Ripper.

Paris designers had been forced to sit up and take notice by the Japanese. What could they do to keep the fashion lead they considered a national birthright? How could they counteract this new approach? What, the cry went up and echoed through the lonely salons of couture, do *we* have that the Japanese do not? How in God's name can we fight back? The answer came slowly and obliquely. Couture – traditional French dressmaking at its highest level – was the thing that Paris had and the Japanese did not. It was right for the times in a way that Japanese austerity was not.

The dazzling advent of Christian Lacroix signalled the *coup de grâce* for Japanese fashion. Almost single-handedly, he put couture back at the top of the fashion agenda, albeit as something to gape at, rather than to buy – a difference that had far-reaching effects. Almost single-handedly, but not quite. Lagerfeld and Yves Saint Laurent were also producing couture collections that put them both at the top of the tree. When the old-established house of

23

Patou launched the inexperienced Lacroix as its designer, what he brought to couture was originality and excess raised to the level of outrage. Outrage is always newsworthy. Clothes that were un-wearable by all but the certifiably insane caught the imagination of the world and made Lacroix's name famous.

Although Lacroix's clashing colours and OTT scale stood on their head the refinement, elegance, balance and understatement that were the traditional strengths of French couture, the press went wild. Each new collection was greeted with greater excite-ment. Lacroix, it seemed, could do no wrong. Everybody wanted to praise him. No one had the courage or foresight to point out how ridiculous his couture appeared. And it did not matter in the slightest. He was the show-stopper, the headline grabber, the Messiah for whom Paris had prayed. Not many people actually bought the clothes, of course, but that was not seen as a problem. It was as if Lacroix had said to Patou's executives, 'Couture is dead. There is nothing newsworthy in it. Let's change both situations and have fun.' They clearly said, 'Go for it!' And he did.

The scam created by his enthusiastic savaging of everything that couture had held most dear was twofold. Suddenly, men who had been proud to be called dress designers felt that this title was no longer appropriate to their dignity. They preferred to be called couturiers, just as their counterparts in the Fifties had. The fact that Dior, Balenciaga and Balmain were exactly that, making their names and money out of one-off clothing, was of no concern to men whose millions came from the impersonal world of mass-market manufacture. It was kudos they were chasing, not historic veracity. All kinds of foolishness resulted. Gianni Versace pro-duced a range with the semantically contradictory label 'Jeans Couture'.

If every designer felt that he could produce a money-spinning line simply by attaching 'Couture' to the label, so every fashion magazine suggested that couture was not to do with an approach to cloth and the body, but was nothing more radical than expensive materials and a plethora of embellishment. Fashionable women believed the myth that everyone could wear couture. They paid a fortune for clothes that were, in essence, merely upmarket ready-to-wear, with a hefty new price tag. But possibly the worst result of the Lacroix couture scam was the undignified scramble by dressmakers to upgrade their frequently unsatisfactory forays into the uncharted waters of high-precision dressmaking which they labelled 'couture'.

The upstart Lacroix was commandeering far too many column inches for other designers to let him hold the field uncontested. The French Empire struck back – as did the Italians and Americans. The toxic fallout from Lacroix went deeper than the clothes. In order to compete, other couturiers mounted their shows ever more extravagantly. Even ready-to-wear designers orchestrated catwalk presentations that took away the breath with their theatricality and elegance. Gianni Versace and Gianfranco Ferre were the two who most entered into the new spirit of freedom, whereby the show became an entity in itself, far removed from the clothes the designers were actually selling. And both were pulled irresistibly – and unresisting – into couture: Versace under his own name, and Ferre for the house of Dior. Couturiers became personalities.

Just as the new couture was not like the old couture, so the new couturier was unrecognisable compared to the old version. Opinions are divided as to Lacroix's worth as a designer, but his effect on fashion was immense. Suddenly everyone talked couture, although few knew exactly what it was. The old rigour of impeccable tailoring was not to be revived – far too demanding. The extravagance of the big ball gowns created in the late Forties and early Fifties was seen as the way forward. Suddenly, in London especially, anyone who knew how to misuse a bolt of stiff taffeta could produce a 'couture' line of ball gowns. Bored housewives, hoteliers, failed actresses – all could have a go and make money out of a gullible but wealthy public.

However, at the same time the professionals in Paris were reviving the true skills of dressmaking. Although they knew that the clothes they were making were more likely to be photographed than bought and worn, couturiers realised the huge potential in publicity that their more outrageously extravagant evening looks could command. Pierre Bergé was not joking when he said that he set Saint Laurent's couture costs against the advertising budget. Everyone wanted a high-profile couture collection. Hugely profitable deals were made, with designers transferring as eagerly as football stars. At Dior, Beatrice Bongibault, at that time managing director, brought in, at an estimated cost of $1.3 million, Gianfranco Ferre. It was an inspired decision. Ferre's collections have proved to be absolutely in the mood of the old couture but not, paradoxically, in the spirit of Christian Dior. Ferre's taste is much more that of Jacques Fath, whose early death from leukaemia in 1954 robbed Paris of one of its greatest talents. His house was reopened last year to coincide with a retrospective of his work, which cruelly highlighted the lack of inspiration in the new set-up.

Couturiers have traditionally held an inflated opinion of their own worth, but the couturier as star was relaunched on the back of the outrageous fantasy happenings of the second half of the 1980s. And he was kept afloat on a sea of words as he found himself giving interviews, guesting on chat shows and making personal appearances. The couturier became showbiz. His views were solicited and he gave them – often with charm, sometimes with wit, but always with alacrity.

To keep fashion perennially alive and of interest to readers, editors and fashion journalists knew that concentrating on frocks that women might wish to buy was simply not enough. Something more exotic was required. 'Give us personalities!' the cry went up.

Who was there to answer the call? Why, the couturier. More fluent than a sportsman, cleaner than a pop star, surely he was exotic enough? Certainly his lifestyle was, in most cases, as far removed from the common light of day as it was possible to get. The extravagantly decorated homes, the costly entertainment, the temperament, the tantrums – what a scenario! But – and here was the rub in the mid-Eighties – how to make the public sufficiently aware?

Irrelevant though Lacroix had made it to modern dress, couture proved to have more pulling power for ordinary people than any other aspect of fashion. Why? Because it was about money, elitism and 'having it all' – the leitmotifs of the decade. It had become a banner in the designer scam. It was a banner meant to convince women that ludicrously padded 'power shoulders', tightly controlled waists and emphasised hips (Lagerfeld even tried to reinstate the padded hips of Dior's New Look) were not fancy dress but essential to sexiness and sophistication.

The 1980s were about the glamour of wealth; the sexiness of money. The new rich wanted to dress the part. Who needed the Japanese approach, stigmatised as the cleaned-up bag-lady look? It was no such thing, of course. Yamamoto and Comme des Garçons collections were masterpieces of refinement. Endlessly beautiful clothes came down their runways – clothes of superb cut and faultless workmanship. But it was too late. Mass fashion had rejected what they had to offer. European couture would eventually turn out to be an irrelevance, but for what came next, no one would look to the East.

'No fuss' dress – aided by developments in heating and transport – brought with it not merely timelessness but also seasonlessness. For centuries, fashion had changed according to the time of year. Summer clothes and colours were abandoned in winter; winter materials and styles were put aside for summer. But that rhythm has gone from fashion for ever. Jeans and T-shirts have no season. As Karl Lagerfeld has said, 'Everybody always needs a clean T-shirt.'

But bread-and-butter clothing robs fashion of one of its major psychological roles, which is to offer, by the changes it brings, the heady possibility of making a new start. Even in these informal days of anoraks and shell suits – both splendidly utilitarian modes of dress – the decorative need cannot be suppressed, which is why even middle-aged and elderly people of either sex are happy to wear them in clashing combinations of acid yellow, livid pink and violent purple.

Of course, no designer ever went broke by underestimating the taste of the public, as the phenomenal commercial success of Gianni Versace shows, and it is a truism that the public can be persuaded of anything if the approach is right. What better proof of this than the creased linen confidence trick played on men and women so successfully in the 1980s? It proved conclusively that even designers crippled by chronic good taste, such as Giorgio Armani, can still make a killing out of the gullible. But the times must be right. And, in the Eighties, they were. The Thatcher man – all bull-headed, Essex thrust and drive – took centre stage. He knew that he had no 'class' but he did not care. He had money and a mobile phone. The world seemed his. Working in totally new fields of communications and frequently servicing artificially created needs, he had no dress precedents to follow except the old-guard elitism of Savile Row. He wanted his own uniform. Italian designers presented it to him in the form of the linen suit. Only the ignorant and uncritical, 'sick of self-love', could have blinded themselves so totally to the squalor of creased and rumpled clothing. It says much for the power of the designer label in the last decade that both men and women allowed themselves to be led by the nose down this particularly unfortunate path.

One of the reasons the designer scam has become so easy is that there are no guidelines to tell *us*, the consumers, when we are being taken for a ride. What can we judge against? In the past, protection was provided by taste. The concept of taste exists only within the concept of what is considered correct in fashion or behaviour at any one time. Rules such as those quoted from Dariaux present either a framework or a strait-jacket, depending upon one's point of view, but they lay down a standard. For centuries, fashion existed within rules. To follow them led to good taste. To ignore them meant you had bad taste.

Taste gave fashion a structure that even the swinging Sixties did not totally undermine. But the Eighties managed to knock it all down. There was the deliberate 'in your face' ugliness of English art school fashion early in the decade and, rather later, the brief glorification of 'sleaze' when designers tried to bring the seedy quality of the sex club and the transvestite bar to fashion. In the early 1990s, we had grunge. All of these exercises in what, by previous standards, was bad taste have been interesting and stimulating. But all were doomed to have a brief and very limited appeal, relying as they did for their effect on a highly sophisticated 'knowing' social and fashion intelligence that few possess. This was bad taste worn in inverted commas, an insider's joke. And it was very confusing. Even apparently worldly fashion journalists who should have been capable of objective analysis threw in the towel and, as a token of their bewilderment and despair, wore badges saying, 'Grunge is ghastly'. They missed the point. Of course it was ghastly – and *that* was the point.

Now that there are no rules of dress to impose taste, it is argued by the old guard that there are no longer any *standards* of dress. It frequently seems that they see Lagerfeld, Lacroix and Versace as the evil trio who have brought about this situation; they shudder at the work of Jean Paul Gaultier and Dolce & Gabbana; they view the deconstructionists such as Martin Margiela, Xuly Bet and Koji Tatsumo as heralding the end of the known fashion universe. Like pre-Christopher Columbus sailors, they long to turn back before we all fall off the edge of the world.

It is a popular fallacy that fashion is some quicksilver creature, endlessly changing and reinventing itself. Rather, it is deeply conservative and resistant to change. To take an example, there are those commentators who see the advent of the so-called deconstructionists as marking a profound change in the nature of fashion. They are wrong, just as they were wrong about the Japanese, the last short-lived shock-horror story almost exactly ten years ago. Raw-edged in every sense, it seemed to herald the end of traditional fashion values but, of course, it did not – and nor will deconstructionism. While these headline-grabbing movements arrive, flourish and die, the real change is taking place elsewhere.

There are two rhythms to fashion, and both behave much as the sea does. The real power of the sea is seen in the heavy, slow-moving swell found in mid-ocean. The waves that beat the shores are quite a different thing. So it is with fashion change. The deep swell of fashion moves slowly, often imperceptibly, and takes time to break upon the shore as a new movement in dress. We all tend to react to the drama of the crashing wave, forgetting it was created far out to sea by a swell of which we on the shore are unaware. What *we* see out in the ocean are the dazzling changes of surface as the sea reacts to variations in wind and light that do not affect – or indeed reflect – what is going on in the deep swell below.

For example, the 1920s seem, in retrospect, to have witnessed a tidal wave in fashion, with hemlines shooting up and waists swooping down in a completely unpredictable way. What a wave! Where did it come from? It seemed without precedent when compared with the heavy-bosomed, serpentine-lined, sweeping-skirted fashion of the Edwardians. But such fashions were merely surface dazzle. The true path of twentieth-century fashion, leading inevitably and logically to the 1920s look, started years earlier, in the previous century, with the advent of rational dress. Yes, the skirts of the rational dress movement reached to the ground. Certainly, placed side by side, rational dress and flapper fashion do not look at all alike. But fashion change is neither governed nor signified by skirt lengths, shoulder treatment or how the waist is emphasised. Change in dress comes with change of attitude.

The rationalists of the 1880s wished women to feel free and healthy in their dress. No more tight lacing, no more boning, no more constriction. They began the swell that led to twentieth-century fashion. Slowly, but inevitably, the swell developed, regardless of all the fun fashion glitter of the Edwardians in clothes that looked back, not forward. World War I began the wave that eventually crashed on the shore in the 1920s, when women had to dress in a way that enabled them to move with ease and perform quite demanding physical tasks. That wave made possible every-thing that has happened since. The New Look, Courrèges' mini, even the flowing garments of the 1970s have all been nothing more than surface glitter. Fashion, in essence – philosophically – has not changed. Rising or dropping hemlines, straight or full skirts, broad or narrow shoulders are transitory variations on the main theme of ease which is what twentieth-century women's clothing has been leading to for the last seventy years.

So has anything of lasting significance happened in fashion since the 1920s? I think yes – and *its* groundswell also started during World War I. The most important change in women's fashion since the flappers has been the development of trousers. Since they made their first tentative appearance in the Twenties they have, admittedly in fits and starts, become an increasingly necessary item in a modern woman's wardrobe. From them have developed jeans, shorts, jogging pants, leg-warmers, leggings, tracksuits and even the much derided shell suit for women.

When, in another hundred years' time, fashion historians wish to characterise the twentieth century, they will think immediately of women in pants. Only then will they recall the decorative dead ends which have given the century such variety and zest: vast Edwardian hats; Thirties flowing crêpe de Chine, bias cut; the New Look in the 1940s; Balenciaga's relaxed silhouette of the Fifties;

Chanel's suits; Courrèges' mini; Yves Saint Laurent's pea jacket; the Japanese avant-garde; power dressing and the new romanticism. And if they wish to illustrate what women were about in the twentieth century, they will choose pictures of Palazzo pyjamas, jeans, Saint Laurent's perfectly cut pants and leg-warmers. If they wish to reflect and philosophise, they will realise that what marks this century out from all others is not only the bifurcated garment but the fact that the shape of female bum – considered dangerously incendiary for eight hundred years – was finally and triumphantly revealed.

Fashion is always moving towards informality. After the confusion of grunge, we have the desperation of deconstruction. Hailed as a deep change, there is little possibility that deconstructionism will resurface in thirty years' time as the wave of the new century. But it is interesting as revealing how fashion can *appear* to change without really going very far. What does this movement actually mean in terms of clothing? To many commentators it seems to have no deeper basis than rudeness in its true sense of 'unfinished': the 'reality' of drifting hems; the 'synthesis' of jeans torn apart and resewn to make a skirt; the 'subversion' of clothes pinned together with safety pins.

Deconstructionism is a philosophical but primarily literary approach to analysis and criticism. It suggests that meaning results, not from what words stand for individually, but from their relation to other words. It questions the assumption that words have intrinsic meaning. So, for example, to understand the Romantic poets we must forget mountains and sea and look at what poetry has gone before them and what has come since. The personalities and attitudes of the poets are nothing. What is important is how one poem progresses from another in a way that makes the author almost irrelevant; at best, merely a cipher. Words refer only to other words. So, literature can only be about literature; the only validity in writing is the writing itself.

What on earth has this to do with fashion? Quite a lot, in fact, but nothing of significance to do with the current wave of deconstructionist designers working in Paris. Surely, history will see their ragbag approach as being devoid of intellectual content. But deconstruction does have a fashion relevance. What it is saying is that clothes can be assessed only within a clothing context; that clothes have no reference point in a social context; that dress validity is only present if clothes are connected to other clothes. A deconstructionist designer will seek inspiration not from the society of the time but by analysis of previous periods of dress – and it must be remembered that deconstructionism is in reality a form of analysis, not of creation.

So we see the fallacy in accepting the nomenclature chosen by Martin Margiela and the group of designers known as the Antwerp Six, which includes Ann Demeulemeester, Jean Colonna and Dries van Noten, all of whom are inclined to heavy breathing when attempting to expiate their sins against fashion in their pursuit of deconstructionism – a term which is already becoming a catch-all fashion word for anything that differs from the highly constructed, traditionally tailored 'power' looks that dominated the late Eighties.

There are people working in fashion who could be considered to have a stance not too far away from the original critical approach of the literary deconstructionists. Vivienne Westwood, fashion's answer to Spinal Tap, and John Galliano, a latter-day Miss Havisham, both draw their inspiration from previous periods of dress. Westwood, in particular, takes the deconstructionist path and cuts away until she reaches the essence, then reassembles with a strong spirit of historic verisimilitude. This does not make her fashion a form of historicism, as Lagerfeld's fantasy forays into the past are, or romanticism, as Ralph Lauren's reconstructions are. Both of those attempt to recreate a society and its attitudes using clothes as their raw material. Westwood and Galliano have a much purer approach, simply using clothes as their inspiration from the past.

And this exposes the flaw in the whole deconstructionist approach. It results in clothes that are totally uncontemporary; clothes that seem like fancy dress; clothes that carry too much weight from the past, too many references to history. But we must be quite clear. *These* are the clothes that result from deconstructionism, not the jumble-sale pickings of the new wave in Paris. Is either a part of the ocean swell, or are both merely glitter on the surface of the sea? Like grunge – which was very much closer to Margiela's deconstructionism than commentators care to admit – neither will have any sufficiently lasting influence on fashion to build into a wave.

As we reach the end of the century, it seems increasingly clear that the source of fashion – or, rather, the source of clothing – is changing. If deconstructionism achieves nothing else, it confirms that what happens in Paris and Milan is increasingly irrelevant to what is worn on the backs of the majority of people in the world. Again, this is part of the fallout of the Lacroix couture revolution, when European fashion turned its back on reality and on judgement: if wearability stops being a criterion for judging clothes, what takes its place is philosophical posturing.

European fashion has lost its way. In their dinner jackets, the ageing men who serve it up look like nothing so much as bank managers or company secretaries. Only Lagerfeld marks himself out by carrying a fan (and in what other world would a fan-toting man be taken seriously?). Camped-up versions of the glamour looks of previous fashion periods are hardly cutting edge. They merely play more or less tasteless variations on a very tired theme. *Women's Wear Daily*'s description of Versace's spring collection for 1992 made clear the lack of original thought: '*Little House on the Prairie* meets the Marquis de Sade'. What is worrying about this is that designers are so unselfcritical and so surrounded by sycophants that they do not realise what is happening. Versace's own description of the same collection was 'The aristocratic cowboy meets baroque . . . jeans and trenches with a fun bit of sado-masochism.'

Couture is busy disappearing up its own arse. Modern European high fashion becomes more and more like modern art – inward-looking, elitist and, most damagingly of all, laughable. As it is rejected by more people, to claw back prestige and relevance, designers are forced to make their ideas even more bizarre.

Star designers have too much money to need to think any more. It is not necessarily money earned from their dressmaking efforts, but money made from the efforts of others selling their name on a wide variety of items, most prominent of which are perfumes. Lacroix was given a free hand at the house of Patou in order to revive their sagging perfume sales; Lagerfeld is backed by the money from Chanel make-up and fragrance sales; Gianfranco Ferre at Dior has his costs covered by the biggest handful of licensees outside Pierre Cardin's empire. None of these men need worry about whether or not his couture and ready-to-wear clothes are worn in any great numbers. Versace's homes, his stores, his publications, his exhibitions and his parties all speak money so loudly that his success cannot be doubted.

High fashion has become an appendix to clothing. Designers, in the main, are attracted to complication in dress with decorative devices that proclaim a sort of prestige by their costliness and irrelevance. They are interested in creating status clothing which might well be inconvenient and uncomfortable, but which is seen by a section of the community as desirable for all that.

But it is not what the majority wants. Clothing that is simple and egalitarian brings its own prestige by association – either with those who stand outside society, alone and strong, such as the cowboys whose image, hopelessly romanticised, permeates the denim and blue jeans culture, or those whom society admires, such as the superheroes of the sports stadium who give credibility to cotton jersey in 'sweats' and work-out gear as well as to Lycra and, most obviously, the footwear of champions. The clothing stimulated by such people has glamour – by association – and this brings its own status.

High fashion is, like the dying year, enjoying a final gloriously colourful autumn that heralds nothing but a winter bereavement. Not that the death is necessarily imminent. With cunning, high fashion – like high art – can be kept going well into the next century.

But ideas must come from somewhere. If easeful fashion based on sportswear is the future, where will the inspiration arise? Most European fashion is of no interest to the twenty-first century and, if there is to be a clear, leading world fashion centre in the future – a premise in itself arguable – it will be New York because that is where the understanding of the new inspirations is to be found. In this, fashion will follow the art scene in the 1950s which swung away from Paris to New York and never returned.

American fashion has always had two sources: home-spun country, and city slicker. In this, it expresses the duality of American cultural life. The Westerner – but not the hillbilly – and the plainsman on one side, and the city man and banker on the other, hold honoured places. American big city fashion, in the hands of Adrian, Mainbocher, Norell, Trigère, Blass and Beene, has reached a level of sophistication and internationalism that rivals most that appears in Paris. Oscar de la Renta, another 'city' fashion designer in New York, is now also designing for the Paris house of Balmain. If items from his own-name New York and Balmain collections became muddled and labels changed, who could tell the difference? Certainly, no one in posterity.

The *real* 'American Look' is casual country dress that has as its inspiration blue-collar rural workers, homesteaders, prospectors and even Pilgrims. Their clothing was developed as *fashion* in the Forties and Fifties by Claire McCardell and Bonnie Cashin and taken up by Lauren, Klein and Perry Ellis in the Seventies. It encompasses denim, footwear, leather and suede and, catching the imagination of the world in the Eighties, it has now begun to oust traditional European fashion as clothing that people actually wish to wear; clothing that they understand; clothing that they are at ease with; but, above all, clothing that brings the wearer, by association, the glamour of the outdoor, sporting world of America. It has even been the inspiration for European designers, most notably Giorgio Armani whose A/X Exchange merchandise has been described as classic American The Gap, with a price tag.

Armani has taken advantage of an interesting cultural collision in the American clothing market. Just as Europe loves America, so Americans love, if not Europe, then certainly Italy. But they also love their own culture. Armani cleverly gives them both with A/X, a range clearly based on American sportswear but done with Italian style – and the label to prove it. And he has hit the jackpot. On 22 February 1993, in a brilliant marketing ploy, eleven outlets of Saks Fifth Avenue, Bloomingdale's and Neiman Marcus opened their instore A/X shops simultaneously: eager, almost fighting, shoppers bought $500,000 worth of T-shirts and jeans in one day. Not surprisingly, Armani intends to milk such a lucrative market for all it is worth. By the end of 1994 he plans to have 150 A/X stores in America. Luca Ramella, chief executive officer of Simint SpA, the company that manufactures the clothes, expects to top $500 million by the end of 1995.

Of course, it is possible to see what Armani does as the most successful scam of all. In essence, his technique with A/X is to take classic items of American sport and casual wear and, barely changing shape or scale, hand them back to us as designer interpretations. His approach is almost a conceptualist one. Like artists who tell us that their work is art and therefore must be perceived as such, Armani seems to be saying of T-shirts and sweats barely distinguishable from their downmarket originals that they are fashion because, by adding his label, they can be seen as nothing else.

3

Pay and Display

We are all used to couturiers as display artists. They are always on parade: high profile, visible, keen to be seen, ready for the action. They have become valued members of the international personality circus. We are so used to reading about them and seeing them on television that it is hard to imagine a time when they were not in demand. They *are* in demand, but usually only because they are famous. The last thing we wish them to talk about is their craft. Too boring by half. We wish them to give us what all international personalities do – anecdotes about other people whose desirability rests on the fact that *they* are famous. We want gossip. Tell us about the models and hairdressers, the customers and photographers, and we will listen. Don't try to preach to us about clothes, please. Remember how we laughed at Vivienne Westwood when she tried to do so on television?

We are so eager to enjoy the designer as personality that we are happy to make designers famous almost before they have shipped their first consignment of clothing. In America, in particular, fame must appear to be instant if it is to be considered valid.

The roll-call of couturiers from the past whose name meant anything at all outside the enclosed world of fashion is a small one. Now, to become famous can take as brief a time as four seasons, and to become a household name is the matter of a few years. This is exactly what happened to Christian Lacroix in the 1980s when a jaded press, delighted by his extravagantly colourful fashion and total disregard of the constraints of taste, gave him the sort of publicity for which only one precedent can be found this century. Christian Dior became famous after two collections and actually appeared on the cover of *Time* magazine, the first couturier to do so. His name became a household word throughout the world, as famous as that of the Pope, General Eisenhower and Churchill, in the late 1940s and early 1950s. But behind his fame stood generations of designers whose names were unknown outside the narrow confines of fashion magazines. Until the swinging Sixties and Mary Quant, the world of fashion was an enclosed one, about which the average man or even woman in the street was totally and happily ignorant.

Dior, Quant, Saint Laurent, Chanel and Cardin – only these five names have achieved a historic profile beyond the confines of the fashion world. Five only out of hundreds of designers and couturiers who have together produced many thousands of garments this century; five only representing the thousands of designers in the rag trade and Seventh Avenue who have designed millions of garments in this century, not even taking into consideration the countless 'little' dressmakers, the 'exclusive' dress establishments, the milliners, furriers, shoemakers and tailors worldwide who were a feature of every city and major town until the early 1960s.

Today, virtually all designers are household names. Giorgio Armani is mentioned on a downmarket soap like *Eastenders* and the producers know perfectly well that the audience will understand the reference. A 'designer' comedy series, *Absolutely Fabulous*, can gear many of its jokes to designer and luxury label names and still command viewing figures of more than 7 million. It is a sign of the success of the designer scam that a world without superstar dressmakers is almost impossible to imagine.

Dress designers became household names in the 1980s because newspapers expanded and, looking for some way to fill their extra pages or hoping to hook into advertising revenue, realised that fashion was a comparatively cheap and easy way to do both. So fashion became newsworthy – or, at least, exploitable. This in itself was not new. Its news value has been reasonably constant throughout the century. In the past, however, it was always seasonal. The couture shows in January and July could normally generate some newspaper coverage and, at times, fashion even reached the front page of publications like the *Daily Mail* and *Daily Express*, which catered for a high percentage of female readers. But the 1980s were different because there was no closed season for fashion. It was treated as news seven days a week, all year round: the latest boyfriend of a top model, the new hairstyle of a glamour princess, the island home of a designer, even the flower arrangement preferences of a make-up artist.

The characteristic of the second half of the twentieth century is intimacy. Increased literacy, and exposure to film (especially through newsreel and TV), have whipped up a fevered interest in the private lives of the great and famous: 'intimate' interviews with film stars and 'exclusive' glimpses into their homes were a magazine staple in the 1930s; books by 'Crawfie', the royal governess, about the 'little princesses' Elizabeth and Margaret sold in their thousands in the late 1940s and 1950s; privileged, insider information has never failed to find eager takers. But the last fifty years have broadened the canvas to include the lives of the new glamour professionals – the super-sport personalities, the pop aristocracy and the international fashion glitterati: the models, photographers and designers who spend so much time appearing at parties across the globe that it is hard to imagine when they actually do the work that made them of interest to us in the first place.

We all delight in insider gossip. We long to get as close as possible to these gilded creatures whose lives are so far removed from our own. What is the lure? Is it their talent that excites us? Is it their wit and wisdom that we crave? The second half of the twentieth century has made the position perfectly clear: the richer the individual, the more glamorous he seems. That is why we gobble up all and any trivia that PRs and the press care to feed us. 'Karl has decided to take a completely new look at women,' a fashion hack writes, and we are hooked immediately.

While Balenciaga was virtually a recluse, now the most important thing for any designer, once he has made his mark, is to be seen and heard as much as possible. His name has to mean something apart from his clothes – a lifestyle, money, glamour, an attitude. The higher the profile, the bigger the sales. Take Armani's shop in Place Vendôme, Paris. A sheikh staying in sixty-four rooms of the Hotel Bristol decided to buy some clothes for the women in his entourage. He phoned the shop, clothes were sent to the hotel and, in a couple of hours, the sheikh had bought over a million dollars' worth. How did he know where to phone? Armani had a profile, built by regular news stories and extremely wide advertising coverage.

Nicholas Coleridge recently pointed out in the *Sunday Times* that 'Designers are not exactly blessed with the world's greatest intellects.' Julie Burchill went even further: 'The fashion industry contains the silliest people in the world,' she said, adding that they were 'the bottom of the barrel'. Both may well be right. But when it comes to getting attention and keeping it, the couture boys operate at a very advanced level. The first thing they realise is that, after a certain point, clothes have little to do with it.

The range of talents on show is remarkable. You want an actor? You've got an actor, from Jacques Fath in the Fifties to Isaac Mizrahi and Todd Oldham in the Nineties. A chat-show star? Take your pick. They all do it, from Lauren in New York to Lagerfeld in Germany, where, just to be more of a polymath than other designer polymaths, Karl has even hosted his own chat show. Not that he is averse to being star guest – a role he fought over with Versace when Italian television did a 'Collections' programme hinged on their different fashion approaches last year. The designer as photographer? Lagerfeld again – he photographs many of the advertising campaigns for the Chanel and Lagerfeld collections and has published a book of his own photographic work, as did Thierry Mugler in the Eighties. The designer as illustrator? Lagerfeld *again* with his book of sketches of fashion's diva Anna Piaggi, and his illustrated version of *The Emperor's New Clothes*. The publishing entrepreneur? Versace and his sister Donatella, who put together *South Beach Stories* with photographs by Bruce Weber and Doug Ordway and short stories by Marco Parma. The establishment figures? Versace and Miyake at the V&A; Armani at the Guggenheim. The lecturers? Karan and de la Renta at the Fashion Institute of Technology, the 'Fashion in Contemporary Living' series, where de la Renta told his audience of idealistic students, 'I got into fashion because I thought I could make a lot of money.' And Oscar thought right, with a sale of $600 million worth of goods bearing his name in 1991.

Even if they themselves are only moderately well off, designers are ideal companions for the truly wealthy. They make marvellous walkers. They are non-threatening. They are clean and well-behaved. Even Jean Paul Gaultier – sometimes referred to as fashion's Bart Simpson – can be relied on to behave infinitely better than the average Sandhurst man when out on a spree. They know everyone and by everyone they are known. And, being largely an unmarried profession, they are available – they will party at the flick of a wine waiter's napkin. And, if necessary they will even lend you a frock.

It is one of the great sadnesses in many designers' lives that society frowns upon them wearing their own creations in public. So the next-best thing is to be photographed standing very close to somebody who *is*. If she is also rich, well connected and a paying customer, even better. So, there is Valentino gallantly supporting the tireless Nan Kempner. Here is Lagerfeld, allowing the air from his fan to cool the brow of Paloma Picasso. There is Yves Saint Laurent, being supported by Catherine Deneuve, as they negotiate their route to a table. There is Versace, holding tight to his sister Donatella – who is wearing his sprayed-on catsuit – in case she misses her footing and her filleted body slides down the nearest grating.

Profile means parties, and like the rest of the fashion world, fashion parties are nothing like they appear. They exist only as occasions to hype something to the millions not invited, and only the most vacuous and uncritical could possibly enjoy them. They are hard work. But the designers can't resist them, and can even make money out of them. One of the *enfants terribles* of the Paris scene, aware of how much of a boost his presence can give a promotion, hires himself out at £10,000 for an evening appearance.

In the opulent 1980s, no Italian designer with an ounce of self-esteem (which in effect means no designer) would dream of letting collection week in Milan go by without throwing a grand party. Most designers in Paris did the same. In London there were fewer parties, but those that there were generated an almost unbelievable level of hysteria – especially amongst the PRs and organisers of London Fashion Week. As a journalist commented, 'They really do believe that it is more important to be seen at the Katharine Hamnett party than it is to see her show.' They were possibly right. Not content with being seen, designers soon came to realise that their parties offered new opportunities to keep tabs on the very press they expected to report their every move. They competed for journalists' loyalties by deliberately issuing clashing invitations. They made the invitation for dinner – sit-down rather than buffet – so that once present, no guest could slink away unnoticed to attend any other event that evening.

But these were parties to die for. Consider the Armani bash in Milan, the most elegant and controlled of them all. Every season, the courtyard of his palazzo in the via Borgonuovo – which is also

Armani's HQ – was transformed into a restaurant with illuminated trees, fabric-draped walls, perfectly appointed tables and satin-covered seats, not just for a couple of dozen, but for hundreds of guests. The food was refined Italian at its best – which means far superior to most French cuisine. Pasta flavoured with sauces of asparagus, wild mushrooms and truffles; smoked salmon; salads tossed in dressing of a refinement that imparted little more than a hint of flavour to the dish; fresh fruit at its prime and private-label wines. Such understated elegance had journalists slavering with anticipation, desperately checking their mail in case the privileged invitation had been withdrawn this season. It also thrilled them because they knew that, however briefly, they had been swept up into the International Big Time where money was secondary and standards were paramount.

In Paris, they ordered things differently. Perfume launches at Versailles were unforgettable experiences done with an élan that would have delighted Louis XIV. But they were not exclusive. The Parisian way of sorting the sheep from the goats was not by a designer dinner in the Milan manner but by something even more desirable: the very small dinner party given in honour of the designer by a well-known society hostess or member of the aristocracy in her *hôtel particulier* . . . Georgina Brandolini gives a party for Valentino at the Palais de Chaillot and invites the likes of Lynn Wyatt, Nan Kempner and Joan Collins. Florence Grinda borrows the beautiful home of her mother, Giselle Michard-Rellissier, for a dinner to honour Ungaro, and her guests include Lynn Wyatt (again!) Jacqueline de Ribes and Shepari Khashoggi.

Rarely more than twenty sat down at these most exclusive of evenings and, for those who did, pecking order was a cause of great concern. Proud the journalist chosen to sit at the maestro's right hand, even though the designer would usually manage to share the pleasure of his company with all of his guests by changing his seat between courses.

45

However, it was London, the least sophisticated of fashion cities and the one with the least money to throw away on entertainment, that arguably scooped them all with its receptions at No. 10, with Mrs Thatcher gritting her teeth at the fatuity of it all and smiling when offered gratuitous insults by guests unprincipled enough to accept invitations from a woman whose political tenets were anathema to them; or the bashes at Lancaster House or Kensington Palace not only with royalty in attendance but with the ultimate world prize – the Princess of Wales – acting as hostess. No wonder American journalists continued to pop into London for so long after their instincts told them that London fashion had slipped quietly into limbo.

But if London had the social cachet, New York is the true spiritual home of the designer party. There they are bigger and better than anywhere else. They can also, surprisingly enough, be quite a lot of fun. European designers – especially the Italians – love them because they are always such naked parades of power. As befits a man whose show signature tune is 'New York, New York', Valentino – always ready to kick up his heels and party – throws his own bashes in Manhattan and, as everyone in fashion knows, what Val does today, Versace does tomorrow . . . and Lagerfeld . . . and Armani. . . . Now they *all* give parties in New York. In fact, it has become impossible for a European designer to step off Concorde and take his limousine to the Hôtel Pierre without it being the immediate signal for the champagne glasses to be polished, the flowers to be arranged and the little gilt chairs to be dusted off. When a foreign designer arrives he is king for a day. He even gets to chat on the Charles Rose show on TV. No wonder he wants a party to put the icing on the cake.

For many designers, the greatest excitement in partying is counting how many women are wearing their creations. There is always a huge fight to dress the stars at the Oscar ceremonies. It is easy to see why. Oscar night can command viewing figures of over a billion.

'If there's a movie star around, you can bet there's an Italian designer not far away,' said *Women's Wear Daily* (*WWD*). One of three Italians, to be exact: Armani, Versace and Valentino battle most fiercely for the honour of dressing the stars. US journalist Liz Smith replied, when asked if designers were a dying breed, 'Could the Oscars exist without Giorgio Armani?' Armani has been king of the ceremony for the last few years and that has not pleased Versace, who said rather primly in 1992 that he did not 'approve of designers chasing actors so they can dress them'. According to *WWD*, he felt it was 'just a way of selling oneself and showing off'. From the man who takes such pleasure in dressing pop stars including Eric Clapton and Elton John – and letting the world know it – this protest rings a little false. But about the selling he is right.

Weeks, even months, of careful negotiations are required to persuade the stars to allow couturiers to lend them a dress – which, it is understood, will frequently not be returned – for the big night. The Beverly Hills shops of the designers come on very strong in their canvassing and are happy to arrange to supply clothes as gifts, or at least at cost, to the chosen star for all manner of occasions, including purely personal, private ones. The dresses are put down to expenses and, indeed, they *are* publicity expenses.

Feathers can fly if an actress changes allegiance. According to *WWD*, Armani and his advisers became very nervous when it was revealed that for the Council of Fashion Designers of America (CFDA) Awards in 1992, Angelica Huston was to be dressed by Calvin Klein and, worse, was to be on his table at the $850 per head gala dinner. Aware that the fashion world viewed Angelica Huston as a committed Armani clothes-horse, they began to put on pressure. Lee Radziwill, working for Armani PR, was reported as being 'difficult' and being 'very, very positive' that she wanted a star in Armani's clothes if he were to host a table at this rather expensive gathering. Gabriella Forte, executive vice-principal of Armani SpA, waded in by suggesting that such an American evening should be reserved for US designers and that CFDA 'should not ask Armani, Chanel and all the rest to buy tables'. The last word came from Donna Karan, who piously claimed that it was wrong to involve the stars 'in this sort of fashion thing, really!'

But only so many photos fit into any magazine; only so many column inches in any newspaper; only so many minutes on any TV channel. One of the best ways to get your share is not by designing better dresses than the next man, but by rubbishing him to anyone who will listen. In this the Italians excel. Fashion's Montagues and Capulets are alive, well and raring for a fight in Milan and Rome. Valentino's right-hand man, Giancarlo Giammetti, crosses swords with anyone he can find who wants a tussle, from home-grown Versace – whom the Valentino crowd consider an upstart – to France's Pierre Bergé, the person behind Yves Saint Laurent. Brave indeed is the person who speaks warmly of Armani to the Versace entourage, and vice versa.

Pierre Bergé, who has had his fair share of criticism, will trade insults with anybody. He has a sharp line in put-downs, his favourite being to forget the name of, say, Ralph Lauren, or to make a judgement such as: 'American designers have absolutely no influence whatsoever.' Lagerfeld is equally fearless. His comments are always amusing because they raise bitchiness to the level of art. After he used Cindy Crawford in a show he exhibited the obsession with size that grips all designers, as well as tossing off a gratuitous insult, when he said that Crawford was 'impressed by the show because she had never done a huge one like this in Paris. Maybe she did Versace, but Versace is a small thing, in a swimming pool' (at the Ritz, in Place Vendôme). Of the Antwerp Six, led by Margiela and Demeulemeester, he commented, 'Those people who nobody can remember their names? . . . I can't tell the difference between one thing and another. Is it on purpose that it all looks the same, or what?'

Even on the rare occasions when designers come together, the sparring does not cease for long. At Convivio AIDS, an Italian fund-raising fair in support of charities in Milan, petulance and prejudice ran completely out of control. It was a latter-day miracle that Armani, Versace, Valentino and Ferre could bear to stand close to each other long enough to be photographed together. Maybe out of gratitude for this, the event was a great financial success, raising $2 million for the charities, despite the fact that while no one was looking 1,200 bottles of champagne and wine were stolen. A good effort by all four men, you might imagine, until you remember that in the same year Versace alone spent $3 million buying a house in fashionable South Beach and admitted that he would need to spend the same amount again to get it how he wanted it. Charity begins at home.

The friendship of the Italian quartet was brief. Versace put things back on their normal footing when he told the press that Valentino's dress for Elizabeth Taylor at a ceremony made her look like Nero's wife Poppea, and that the jeans and jacket he supplied for her to attend a concert were much better. Giancarlo Giammetti pointed out in reply that the house of Valentino thought Miss Taylor looked better as a woman than a cowboy. Journalists reported that both houses were discomforted by the fact that at the Council of Fashion Designers of America awards ceremony in 1993, Armani, due to present an award to Donna Karan, milked the loudest and longest applause of the evening. The enmity continues. If Armani holds a party during Milan collections at the Rolling Stone nightclub, Versace does the same at the City Square nightclub. Guest lists are anxiously scanned, budgets hastily increased and plans rapidly adapted in the fight to keep ahead.

Armani not only imported 20,000 roses from Marrakesh for his Rolling Stone party, he also invited Suzanne Bartsch and a team of transvestites to enliven the evening. Versace, not to be outclassed, turned City Square into a downtown New York disco with banks of video monitors near the entrance showing an endless loop of advertisements. He also had a barbershop, tattoo parlour, hot-dog and pretzel stands around which break-dancers, rappers and graffiti artists fought for space.

If the column inches devoted to these events are not forthcoming, there are ways to overcome the problem. For example, Calvin Klein placed 116 pages of advertising in one issue of *Vanity Fair*. But the best answer is to go one step further – for *Vanity Fair* read vanity publishing. The designer publication – tightly focused and completely uncritical, written and produced under house supervision – is not about anything as overt as selling clothes. It is to do with spreading the word, creating the image, developing the aura.

Le Magazine de Chanel costs the firm $300,000 and it appears to be not even trying when compared with the drop-dead swank of Italian designer 'catalogues'. It seems a demeaning term for such luxurious productions, but that is what they are: catalogues, not for showing the new merchandise but for brainwashing us into believing that the designer is a sensitive, creative type – a man in touch with the great artistic movements of his time. Italian designer catalogues are actually sexy collectors' items starring top models – Claudia Schiffer, Helena Christensen, Naomi Campbell – photographed by the greatest and most expensive photographers – Irving Penn, Steven Meisel, Patrick Demarchelier – in the most exotic locations from Cap Ferrat to secret coves in the Caribbean. Isabella Rossellini and Monica Bellucci, moodily black and white for Dolce & Gabbana; Naomi Campbell in full-colour tartiness for Versace; Amber Valletta and Patricia Arquette coolly distant for Armani.

And what the Italians do the Americans do just as well, because all that is needed is a minimum of $100,000 in order to buy the best. But it is possible to do so much more. The Ralph Lauren publicity of the last ten years has created an attitude of mind for millions of people who flick through the pages of his patrician advertising. Nothing as vulgar as commerce will be found there. These are not practical pages for those keen to rush out and buy. There are no sizes, no prices, no details of colours or materials. Instead, the pages show us a way of looking – at the world and at ourselves. The carefully contrived object is to give the impression that we are perusing family photograph albums featuring people, not models. The models are chosen precisely because they look 'real', and include the full family range from grandfather to junior in the supporting cast who, as in a Bernini sculpture, gather round and lift on high the icons to which our attention must be drawn. The young men have class and character, rather than beefcake sex appeal; the women are pure, refined and, could they speak, their voices would be quiet and subdued. There is nothing strident in this make-believe world where the lawns and lakes look as if they have been there for ever; the library furniture is rich mahogany that picks up the gleam from the leather-bound tomes; and the tea is served on bone china with the family silver on display.

What Lauren gets is profile by association. When you see the situation, you imagine him in it. This, the catalogue says, is how Ralph lives. This is glamour. Class is the message, and it is only after you have achieved the *mise-en-scène* that you are expected to start thinking about buying the clothes. Any head of a totalitarian state would sacrifice a few firing squads to be given the skill (and money) for mind manipulation that Lauren advertisements exemplify.

The Lauren catalogues present pictures without words – a genre of which fashion designers are very fond. The *books* sponsored and paid for by designers do have some words, always perfectly placed on their elegant pages, and are usually either banal or pretentious. The mood was set a long time ago with the publication of Issey Miyake's *East Meets West* in 1978, a 'hold your breath in the holiest of holies' series of pictures by top photographers with commentary by Japanese intellectuals on the grandest of philosophical concepts such as 'Man and his Clothing' or 'The Form of Cloth'.

This was followed in 1983 by Miyake's *Bodyworks*, which accompanied an exhibition that travelled the world and displayed his clothes less as fashion than as works of art. Miyake's garments were put on show not in shops but in museums and art galleries, including the Victoria and Albert. The *Bodyworks* book pulled in some of the cultural, artistic and intellectual gurus of the time, including Andy Warhol, Miles Davis, Lily Auchincloss, Maurice Bejart, Christo, Milton Glaser and Ettore Sottsass. Everyone, it seemed, wished to be part of the Miyake magic.

In the 1980s, endless designer picture books rolled off the presses. Produced to the highest standards, elegantly designed and using the work of the world's top photographers, they were the bimbos of the publishing world, beautiful but dumb. They followed the Miyake formula – a page or two of purple prose from the editor of an influential fashion magazine, preferably American; a few quotes about the foolishness of fashion from intellectuals of the past, Montesquieu being perennially popular; a comment from an internationally famous architect or a writer or two. The trend has continued into the 1990s with Valentino's *Thirty Years of Magic*, published to the highest standard by US publisher Rizzoli; and Versace's catalogue *Signatures*. Both are magnificent examples of vanity publishing, image-making exercises of the utmost grandeur. It took Franco Moschino to send up the genre with his luxury volume, *X Anni di Kaos!*, in which he exposed such blatant narcissism. Nevertheless, it is that image which sells the frocks that make the millionaires. But there are other ways of doing it.

In 1985, press at the Armani shows were given discreet, cream paperbacks with the words 'Giorgio Armani' printed in black on the cover. No pictures, no clues as to what these books were about until they were opened and journalists read 'Rassegna Stampa' (press review). The comments of all the major journalists from Italy, Germany, France, Great Britain and the United States were presented unedited and without comment. These elegant little books became a feature of the Armani show for several years and they never failed to puzzle journalists, who were incapable of knowing whether their words had been collected as a 'thank you' by Armani or as the equivalent of 'must try harder'. It ensured that Armani received some of the most thoughtful consideration in the press – and some of the longest reviews.

The books were not only a brilliant publicity coup. By presenting last season's comments at this season's show, Armani gave his *oeuvre* a sense of continuity and seriousness that made it seem much weightier than mere projections of clothing for six months hence. He seemed to be saying, 'I am an artist, this is my body of work – an ongoing investigation – and you are the critics filing interim reports. Read your words and, if wisdom dawns and you have to eat them, learn by your mistakes.'

The press allowed him to get away with murder. Comments such as, 'I do not design for a face, or with a person in mind – what I have in mind is the quality of their spirit', should have been laughed out of court. Even the statement: 'The deep morality, the sainthood, is limited to Giorgio Armani. Mary Magdalene is Emporio – with it I do business', was received without question.

Just as Lauren has made himself the fashion world's archivist, so Armani has commandeered the intellectual high ground. The resultant publicity and sales have become legendary, but canny Armani does not rely on words alone. At the same time as the 'Rassegna Stampa' booklets appeared – small and understated – he initiated Milan's answer to Times Square with his vast Armani Wall in via Broletto. The side of a five-storey building, it was painted with Brobdingnagian figures showing the new Armani look. Changed twice-yearly to coincide with the arrival of press and journalists for the Milan collections, it exemplifies Armani's understanding of the fashion world. There is, he realises, only a certain amount of mileage in words. Images speak volumes – and the bigger the better. It is no accident that every taxi from the airport to the centre of town, laden with eager fashion folk, drives along via Broletto – the Milanese are as proud of their boy as he is of himself. They view his bone-dry creations as the sartorial equivalent of Henry Moore's sculptures.

For the classic example of the couturier with profile we need look no further than another Italian. Is it because *WWD* dubbed him 'The Chic' that Valentino Garavani always smiles? Or is it because he is a billionaire, with homes in Rome, New York, London, Gstaad and Capri, all crammed with antique furniture, the walls heavy with Picasso, Monet and Matisse, the floors richly carpeted with the finest Aubusson?

Valentino is a man for whom the term VIP might have been invented, so smoothly does he cross frontiers and move from continent to continent, followed (and more importantly preceded) by a hand-picked entourage whose sole job is to ensure that the rites of passage are accomplished with the minimum of fuss. Absolutely nothing is allowed to ruffle the maestro's beatific existence, anywhere in the world.

Is that why Valentino smiles – or is it the fact that when he arrives at any of the world's fashionable watering holes he is immediately known and fêted by all? He is a friend of every important woman in the fashion world, from Jackie O. to Nan Kempner. He is not just welcomed at every fashionable bash in Paris, New York or LA – his attendance is eagerly solicited, because it is understood that if Valentino appears, the party has been given a benison quite as powerful as one from that other exalted denizen of Rome, the Pope. In fact, it is arguable whether or not the likes of Susan Gutfreund or Gloria von Thurn und Taxis would choose the pontiff rather than the dressmaker, given the choice.

Valentino Garavani, it is clear, strolls through the grass of Parnassus as one who has been mightily favoured by the gods. But the gods do not shower their blessings with prodigality. They have to be earned. And Valentino *has* earned them – in spades. How has he – the little Italian boy from quite humble middle-class origins – become one of the elect, known across the world as one of the fathers of Italian fashion who has even been able to get away with adapting the 'Made in Italy' trademark to read 'Made in Valentino'?

Valentino has made his name and his fortune by steering clear of originality. He has always opted to work within the parameters imposed by the fashion lore of the moment. He has never introduced a new shape or altered a skirt length. By being predictable, he has not only become rich, he has earned the sort of loyalty that ensures that his customers stay with him. Like Oscar de la Renta, Geoffrey Beene, Bill Blass, Givenchy or Jean-Louis Scherrer, Valentino's secret is to create ravishingly beautiful gowns that are immedate 'must haves' for the rich, and instantly covetable by the rest. He is claimed as a friend by women who would never dream of questioning the bill.

The Roman audience at a Valentino show in the mid-1980s was simply extraordinary. The Queen of the Night, for whom even Valentino would delay his start, was Sophia Loren – the siren who had given all Italian women in the audience an identity which was to be clothed and made elegance personified by Valentino himself. Lesser stars such as Gina Lollobrigida and Claudia Cardinale circled around her, driving the paparazzi mad with excitement as they pretended not to be able to find their seats, though everyone knew that the legendary Valentino courtesy and efficiency always ensured that every guest was personally conducted to her place.

But the real coup was the way in which Valentino pulled in the Italian aristocracy, those aloof beauties whose exclusive world would open like a flower to the sun for a friend. Crespi, Brandolini, Cicogna. . . . Then the queens . . . Sofia of Spain, Noor of Jordan . . . the *principesse* . . . Maria Gabriella of Savoia, Firyal of Jordan . . . the Aga Khan family. . . . Then the Europeans . . . Windisch-Graetz, Thyssen-Bornemisza, von Fürstenberg, Rothschild . . . the guest list at Valentino is always as heavy with titles as the Almanack de Gotha. And Our Val (as *Women's Wear Daily* dubs him) loves them all – just as Val's Gals love him.

What always distinguished a Valentino couture show from the rest in Rome was the legs of the private customers. Row upon row of perfection, these were legs that never had to walk – unless they chose to; legs that had been expensively coaxed and wheedled into their prime in all those exclusive clinics in the high lands of Europe: the woods of Bavaria, the mountains of Switzerland, the Dolomites and the Pyrenees . . . all lightly crossed, waiting for the maestro to reveal his dreams made reality for his ladies this season.

Gold Cartier pens poised, Val's customers were ready to mark, with a discreet cross on their programme, the choices that they would have Valentino make up for them; the choices that would enable them to face the coming season with the knowledge that on their backs they would display the incontrovertible proof of their power, wealth, taste and, above all, their breeding.

As they discreetly applauded his efforts at the end of the show, the hall would resound to the clash of gold on gold as bracelets became intertwined. Then the maestro would appear. As he walked down the catwalk, immaculate, unruffled, smiling, those hooded eyes taking in the minutest reactions on the all-important front row, they would rise in a body to give him the applause his fashion aplomb so richly deserved.

Life has been kind to Valentino. He has avoided the pitfall of becoming *démodé*. He knows that if you are never at fashion's cutting edge, you are unlikely to be supplanted. He once told me, without a trace of arrogance, 'I know *everything* about couture. Everything.' And he does. It is not for nothing that Jackie Onassis said, 'Valentino, live for ever!'

4

Buying and Selling

Fashion is a commercial, industrial art, concerned less with beauty than with making money.

Its influence on the economics of a country is immense, as strong in the powerful capitalist nations of the West, who are normally consumers as well as manufacturers, as it is in the developing countries where the vast majority of the sweated labour make clothes for some of the West's most prestigious designer labels with no hope at all of ever becoming consumers themselves. Should the whole edifice of fashion come crashing down, there would be serious economic effects far beyond the grand temples of couture in Paris, Milan and New York.

But even in the face of recession, the fashion world has come up with stratagems to keep itself alive at a time when its traditional customers are under financial pressure. The priority has to be selling clothes, but buying them involves much more from the public than buying smaller, more intimate items such as make-up or jewellery. There is a rite of passage. After the selection from the rails comes the all-important commitment of entering the changing room, undressing and trying on. This is a considerable psychological hurdle when money is tight. So, too, is the embarrassment many people still feel when trying on clothes. More than most shoppers, fashion consumers must feel a commitment to buy if they are to be persuaded to take their own clothes off and put new ones on. That is one of the reasons designers set so much store by profile and media coverage: it can help build up that commitment to their name and their products.

By overpricing its goods, the fashion business guards itself against the psychological barriers to buying that arise whenever money is short, so that the good times bring enough into the kitty to enable the business to ride out the bad. Those designers who have the nous to keep control of an empire also have their name tied to a range of cosmetics or a perfumery line. In times of recession, these lines sell well: they are cheaper than clothes, do not involve the same psychological buying problems, and are easy ways for women to cheer themselves up. In some cases, they are the only way fashion houses have kept going. There are whole areas in a fashion empire that do not always make great amounts of money or even manage to cover their costs – French *haute couture* being one such case. In the 1990s, no couture line can continue without having behind it a huge perfume empire or a complicated infrastructure of licensed firms providing different luxury objects to defray the losses.

Fashion is no longer simply about making frocks. It is about business management. More and more, fashion has spread its risks as widely as possible. Although experience has shown more than once that efficiency and increased profits do not automatically come with a wide range of business interests, the belief in diversification inspired the movement that swept through the world of luxury and high fashion goods in the second half of the 1980s. It led to the buying up of the grand old names in couture and the amalgamation of various companies to tap into the kudos and the cash that the top names could generate.

Even though there were safer ways of investing their money big businessmen queued up to get in. Glamour was the one sure-fire commodity that the fashion world could be relied upon to deliver with a style that not even Hollywood could guarantee. For the men in suits who spent their lives poring over balance sheets it had the force of the most powerful aphrodisiac known to man. It tempted normally sober banks and finance houses to back the fashion powers with huge amounts of money.

It was not merely the joy of sitting in the front row at the fashion show of the house you owned; it was not the sexiness of being part of the high camp world of supermodels; it was not even the social excitement of finding yourself entertaining the likes of Princess Caroline of Monaco. It was an amalgam of all these things – and more.

The fashion world also gained from its association with the financiers. It found them sexy. What attracted was the power of the enormous wealth they controlled. Fashion houses were prepared to enter into a symbiotic relationship with the big-money boys, provided that they did not attempt to interfere with anything artistic. And, as long as the money was pouring in, the arrangement was attractive to both sides – at the beginning.

Most renowned of the new breed of fashion magnates is the Frenchman Bernard Arnault. Though some fashion people like to cast him as the big, bad wolf who gobbled up the Red Riding Hoods of traditional couture, it seems unfair to condemn him just because he was much better at it than anyone else.

Arnault, a property developer, came unheralded out of the provincial mists, but far from being a yahoo, he is a studious and artistic man whose greatest form of relaxation is playing the piano, usually Chopin. Arnault possessed that most criticised of business traits: burning ambition that blazed forth, frightening or exciting everyone who knew him.

His first step was to gain control of the vast but ailing textile company Boussac, which had originally backed Christian Dior when he had first opened his own-name salon and startled the world with the New Look in 1947. Arnault wanted Dior because, even though it had long lost the lustre of its great days of the Forties and Fifties, and its clothes were considered old-fashioned, no fashion house in the world had a wider network of licensees who paid the company money in order to produce goods of their own design but bearing the most prestigious fashion name in the world.

Of over 260 licences for fashion items, including stockings, scarves and jewellery, the most lucrative was that for sunglasses which was worth over FF 300 million per year. These licences kept the house of Dior afloat despite the dire performance of its fashion. Even Pierre Bergé, chairman of Yves Saint Laurent, and a man as single-minded in his pursuit of business goals as Arnault, had shown interest in amalgamating his fashion house with Dior. Like Arnault, he knew that the Dior name was potentially priceless.

When the Boussac empire had collapsed in 1978, it was bought out by the Willot brothers to become part of the Agache-Willot empire. This group also ran into financial trouble in 1981. Propped up by the French government because of its importance to the economy, Agache-Willot lasted until 1984, when it was again in difficulties. This time there were quite a few people ready to take the responsibility off the government's shoulders, including Bernard Arnault and his partner Pierre Godé. They were outsiders to an almost laughable degree but they faced the opposition like latter-day versions of Jack the Giant Killer. Barely known in Paris, their names did not feature in bright lights on the Bourse: it was as if their very provincialism gave them courage to set out on a task that to all but madmen or visionaries would have seemed as preposterous as a Pekinese trying to rape a Great Dane. The Agache-Willot empire, for all its troubles, had a yearly sales sheet worth over ten times that of the Arnault business. Arnault showed his business flair by deciding that, rather than wait for the government to choose from its list of candidates (a list on which he was unlikely to feature), he would deal directly with the brothers, who were, like him, from northern France and as hard-headed, practical and unromantic as he.

A series of James Bond-type secret meetings between Arnault and the brothers in places as unlikely as provincial airports began to swing things Arnault's way. The Willots were reluctantly forced to face the fact that he had outmanoeuvred them. He bought 20 per cent of their shares, 'borrowed' the rest to secure the voting rights that went with them, and had his deal ratified by the government. It was the first step towards control of the biggest empire that the luxury goods and fashion world had seen, comprising some of the biggest marques in Paris.

Arnault's first battle was with the fashion house of Patou who employed Christian Lacroix – a designer who could not have presented a greater contrast to Marc Bohan, the conservative, refined couturier at Dior whose clothes were a byword for good taste and wearability. Lacroix had been given his head at Patou to be as outrageous as possible. Taste and wearability were simply not part of his equation. All that the Patou directors required of Lacroix was that his collections should be sufficiently newsworthy to catch the headlines, thus ensuring that the name of Patou and its perfumes, headed by the legendary Joy, should be kept prominently before buyers who had no intention of ever entering a couture salon.

As a designer Lacroix was essentially bourgeois and provincial – as Christian Dior had been. Perhaps that was the reason why Arnault wanted him to take the place of Bohan. But, like Christian Dior in 1947, Lacroix – or rather, his shrewd business adviser, Jean-Jacques Picart – could not be wooed along these lines. Instead of being the designer at Dior, he wanted his own house. Arnault, to the amazement of the fashion world, gave it to him. The cost was reputedly an initial outlay of FF 70 million and a further investment of over FF 200 million over the next five years.

Patou immediately instigated legal proceedings against what they saw as blatant poaching of their designer, even though their contract with Lacroix did not constitute a long-term commitment. Arnault lost the court case but effectively he had won. He had the hot ticket, and he had him quickly, before the hot ticket became a cold potato. He capitalised on the media excitement over Lacroix by initiating a range of accessories using his name, because he was convinced not only that they would sell off the back of Lacroix's attention-getting collections but also that they were easier to produce than a complete ready-to-wear line, which was still the dream of Lacroix and Picart.

The Patou affair sounded the warning bell in Paris. Such ruthless tactics might well be commonplace in business, but the fashion world expected a little more finesse. It was not to get it. Arnault was unstoppable. Céline – the prestigious high-class leather goods firm, owned by the Vipiana family, which had five shops in Paris and eighty franchised retail outlets around the world – was swallowed up at bewildering speed. Within three months of beginning negotiations the Vipiana were no longer connected with the firm. In 1988 the Tribunal de Commerce of Paris rapped Arnault's knuckles over the Patou affair, and ordered him to pay FF 10 million as an advance against total damages still to be finalised. Lacroix and Picart escaped without taking any of the blame. Lacroix was so much fashion's darling that nobody had heart or courage to take him to task. But the fact is that he was too eager, too much in a hurry, too greedy for fame, and there are many in Paris who have watched with a certain malicious pleasure the eventual disintegration of Arnault's investment in Lacroix. Although Lacroix and his highly original design approach have remained of interest, his importance as a fashion figure is weakening with each season. What shocked and delighted in the mid-1980s seems rather jejune and crude as the mid-1990s approach. Lacroix's name and the reputation of Arnault as a shrewd judge of staying power are being questioned with greater openness now – especially since C'est la vie!, Lacroix's perfume, conceived to recoup Arnault's investment, seems unlikely to make a significant place for itself in the fragrance marketplace.

Having control of Christian Dior gave Arnault the kudos he required. But he had set his heart on also acquiring Parfums Christian Dior, not only to give added lustre to his expanding quiver of prestigious names but also because the firm was a money-spinner invulnerable to the ups and downs of the fashion world. It was a quite separate business from the fashion house of Christian Dior although, as chairman of Dior Couture, Arnault had a seat on the board. Parfums Dior were part of the Moët-Hennessy group under the chairmanship of Alain Chevalier.

With sales of FF 3.2 billion in 1987, Parfums Christian Dior was a prize, even by Arnault's standards. The Christian Dior fashion company could only notch up sales of FF 600 million. Arnault set out to change the situation, helped by a relaxation in the French laws concerning takeovers. But things were already moving at Moët-Hennessy. Henry Racamier, chairman of the prestigious French luggage company, Louis Vuitton, had suggested a merger of the two companies in 1986 but had been repulsed. Undaunted, he went ahead and bought the champagne and perfume group, Veuve Clicquot, owners of Parfums Givenchy which, as a result of the success of its women's perfume, Ysatis, launched in 1984, was showing sales figures of FF 266 million by 1986. Then he returned to Moët-Hennessy; a merger finally took place in 1987 and LVMH, Moët Hennessy Louis Vuitton, was formed.

Internal squabbles and disagreements in LVMH soon tore the company apart and the two main protagonists, Henry Racamier and Alain Chevalier, were at daggers drawn, so much so that Racamier finally arranged a meeting with Bernard Arnault. Arnault was about to take the final giant step that would make him the Emperor of Fashion and give him control not only of Christian Dior and Lacroix but also of Parfums Givenchy. It was a control won only after the most bitter of boardroom battles with Racamier, which left Arnault in charge of LVMH. Ousted from LVMH after a long-running battle with the very man he had called in to help, a battle that had contained elements of farce and melodrama as well as a sinister darkness worthy of *The Duchess of Malfi*, Racamier was left in charge of Lanvin. Chevalier – another victim of the

LVMH siege – got the less than healthy house of Balmain. Arnault became chairman of LVMH on Friday, 13 October 1989. He was now also chairman of Christian Dior, Christian Lacroix, Givenchy, Moët et Chandon, Veuve Clicquot, and Louis Vuitton. It had been a busy five years.

But as the grey Nineties develop, Arnault and many of the businessmen who emulated him must now be wondering whether or not it was worth all the intrigue and effort to hang an albatross around their necks.

LVMH was not the only victim of the luxury fashion trades of Paris as the recession began to bite. Look, for instance, at what happened even to a partnership as powerful as Yves Saint Laurent and Pierre Bergé, who lost control in 1993 of the firm they had founded together in 1961, when they sold YSL to Elf-Sanofi, the pharmaceutical and cosmetic division of the French state-run oil conglomerate, Elf-Aquitaine. Although far from unhealthy, profits at YSL were losing momentum in the early 1990s. Using government money, as a part of a state industry, in 1993 Elf-Sanofi bought 100 per cent control of YSL Scent and Beauty and 90 per cent control of YSL Couture, including furs and ready-to-wear, though Bergé and Saint Laurent retained 90 per cent of the voting rights. Sanofi president, Jean-François Dehecq, predicted a 200-million-franc profit by the end of 1994.

It remains to be seen whether Dehecq's optimism is well founded. Elsewhere, the ruthlessness of men intent on making money has caused some terrible shocks in the fashion world and forced designers to ask whether the security of multibillion-franc backing is not outweighed by the fact that, with such amounts at stake, there is no security at all. Even the most prestigious or amenable designer takes second place, and becomes little more than a hired hand even if the company does bear his name.

It is a pattern that has been repeated throughout the fashion world, once finances are controlled by men who do not understand fashion and see clothes – no matter how exquisite – as just another commodity. For them, the equation is simple. If the commodity fails in some way, the man responsible for the failure must go.

Take the case of New York designer Halston in the 1970s. The fashion business has not forgotten the treatment that this designer was forced to accept when he began to lose control of *his* business. Although it can be argued that his cocaine addiction made it increasingly difficult for him to cope with daily problems, one of America's greatest design geniuses was squeezed out by people who had only one consideration in their heads: profit. They were even prepared to use designs created by other talents but bearing the Halston label. The final indignity was when Halston was locked out of his own business premises in New York's prestigious Olympic Tower.

He was not the only designer to be treated in such a cavalier manner. The same thing happened to André Courrèges in 1985. Courrèges had been the enfant terrible of Paris in the 1960s, along with Pierre Cardin. Both men made their name with 'space age' collections which the press considered fabulous, but which left customers slightly less enamoured. Cardin's vast spread of business interests, which have earned his house the name The General Store, has generated enough money to make him invulnerable to changes in taste or financial climate. Courrèges lacked Cardin's business acumen and entrepreneurial flair, and ended up having to sell control of his fashion house to the Japanese ready-to-wear firm, Itokan, who agreed to support the loss-making couture side of the business. The money continued to flow down the drain. In 1985 the couture side of Courrèges' business was closed, with virtually no consultation. Courrèges was aghast and went on strike in order to gain public sympathy. This he achieved in a way that could only happen in Paris where, even today, couture is considered the single truly artistic form of dressmaking. Everybody, including the French government, which thought that

Itokan had given a promise to maintain Courrèges' couture, was shocked – but powerless because Courrèges had signed away control to the Japanese firm.

These things also happen in Italy. The Milanese designer, Luciano Soprani, found himself at odds with his partners in 1992 when things went wrong between him and Onward Kashiyana, who owned 70 per cent of his company. He filed suit to regain control of his trademark and name from Kashiyana, having the right to use neither once he had split with the firm. The problem was the usual one: lack of money and falling sales had made his backers nervous. When Kashiyana bought a 40 per cent stake in Soprani SpA in 1986, they paid 200 million lire. In a firm with profits from sales around 40 billion lire, it was a good investment. But part of the deal was that Soprani lost personal control of production, which was moved to Kashiyana-owned factories. According to Soprani, the results were catastrophic; quality dropped dramatically and as much as 45 per cent of factory production was never shipped to retailers. By 1991, sales were down to 20 billion lire and Soprani SpA was facing the possibility of an annual loss of 5–6 billion lire. As Soprani told *Women's Wear Daily*, he felt that the downfall of his firm was a direct result of his association with people who understood neither him nor his clothes. He talked of 'the series of circumstances that made me change my style. I wasn't the same any more. I felt like I was being conditioned.'

Soprani was left impotent while the case continued, unable to use his own name, just as New York designer, Bill Kaiserman, had been when his arrangement with Kashiyana had gone sour. But the saddest and most notorious example of how ruthlessly backers can treat creators, when money is at stake, is that of Jean-Louis Scherrer. For contracted designers to be dismissed without warning and with no explanation is not unusual in Paris. What made the Scherrer case an instant *cause célèbre* was the fact that

Scherrer was no hired hand. In December 1992, at the age of 56, Scherrer was evicted from the fashion house he had founded thirty years before and in which he still had a 10 per cent financial stake. Apart from boardroom battles – no out-of-the-way thing in the fashion business – he was given no warning before the day he arrived in his office and found a tersely worded letter of dismissal on his desk. To add insult to injury, he had been sacked in the most damaging way: under the most serious French legal heading, 'Faute lourde', which means culpable dereliction of duty. As Scherrer said, he was made to feel about as important to his own-name company as a street sweeper. His severance pay was one month's salary.

Scherrer had never been one of the great money-spinners like Yves Saint Laurent, but he was a successful couturier with a world reputation. Financial disagreements in the 1970s had caused him to split with his majority shareholders Orlâne, and he bought back from them full rights to his name. In 1990 he sold a 90 per cent stake in his company to Ilona Gestion, a holding company majority controlled by Seibu Saison with Hermès as a major backer. They invested FF 78 million in the company which, immediately prior to their involvement, had made a profit of FF 5 million. Their plan was to inject another FF 25 million before the end of 1993 but, in exactly the same way as at Soprani, things went wrong and a reasonably healthy balance sheet soon plummeted into the red.

In 1990 the firm of Jean-Louis Scherrer lost FF 25 million. In 1991, the loss was 42 million. As Patrick Thomas, president of Scherrer and managing director of Hermès, said, these were 'unsustainable losses'. He brought in Erik Mortensen from Balmain to design the collection and began to rationalise the firm by sacking sixty-five employees, who joined Scherrer's daughter and muse Laetitia, who left the company in May 1991. Scherrer sued Groupe Hermès and Seibu Saison for FF 200 million damages and Ilona Gestion has demanded the right to have its 1990 acquisition annulled. The firm is determined to get back the FF 100 million it has already paid out and is asking for FF 78 million in damages. The case rumbles on.

The new corporate shape of the fashion world has yet to be seen in its entirety. The future direction of the business is unsure, with the huge conglomerates possibly proving too unwieldy for the adaptability that is the prerequisite of the fashion world. What *is* certain is that the future will be upon us sooner than we think.

Most of the top designers – the ones shops trust and rely on for putting money in the bank – are old. Yves Saint Laurent is 58; Karl Lagerfeld is 55, Giorgio Armani 59, Ralph Lauren 55, and Valentino 62. Even the second wave is getting on. Gianni Versace is 48, Donna Karan 46, Claude Montana 47, Jean Paul Gaultier 42, Christian Lacroix 43, Franco Moschino 44 and Romeo Gigli 45.

The young Turks – John Galliano at 33, Marc Jacobs at 31, Todd Oldham 32, Koji Tatsumo 30 – have by no means convinced the public that they have the staying power to swing fashion into the next century. For all his talent, Galliano's career has been peppered with financial problems; Marc Jacobs had a difficult time with the Perry Ellis label. How secure can any young designer feel in the 1990s? There are so many pitfalls, so few guarantees. And it all takes so long. Anna Sui, currently one of the darlings of Seventh Avenue (S.A.), has taken twelve years to make a breakthrough of any significance. She had her first runway show in 1991 and her wholesale revenue for 1992 was a mere $1.7 million. To call such figures inadequate may seem strange, but money like that can disappear in a season, leaving a designer either bankrupt or facing the fact that his or her credit rating is nil. Another American designer, Todd Oldham, has taken even longer to make the grade. He started out with his mother in Dallas in 1980 when he was only 18, yet it is only in the last four years that his name has meant anything in fashion circles beyond S.A.

Reaching the top in fashion has often been long and hard.

Today's business focus on short-term profits makes it even more difficult to take a chance on an unknown designer. There are no overnight successes. Talent, luck and money are not enough. What is also required is persistence – and publicity. And in a classic 'Catch 22' situation, much of the publicity goes to the older, already established designers.

Whereas the fashion world is, on one level, remarkably generous, on the top level it is intolerant of all but the very best. Looking at the younger talents, it is not easy to see who will be the Lagerfeld of 2020. In 1992, *Women's Wear Daily* carried a feature on young designers in Paris. Called 'Who's New', it mentioned Carlos Rodriguez, a Venezuelan who learned his trade with Cardin, Scherrer and the Italian ready-to-wear manufacturers. It looked at an American, John Speight, who had studied at the Mayer School; Christophe Lemaire – ex-Mugler, Yves Saint Laurent and Lacroix; and Sylvie Skinazi, also from Lacroix. Good backgrounds, impeccable training, in the right city, they could all have a chance. But in order to do so, they must be *given* the chance; that is the responsibility of the money men, in whose interests it is to guarantee their future profits. When the chance comes, the young designers must grab it. And they must get it right.

The story of Robert Merloz haunts all aspiring designers. Merloz got his chance on the grandest scale when he began in 1992, with Pierre Bergé as fairy godmother and backer and even a good-luck smile from Yves Saint Laurent himself, according to the press. His first show bombed, with not one outfit raising any applause – an unheard-of thing at a début. Clothes bought by Barneys of New York in the hope of getting Yves Saint Laurent Rive Gauche as part of the deal were returned when it became apparent that Rive Gauche would not follow. Merloz was the victim less of his talent than of Parisian politics. He was seen as an upstart, a Bergé favourite. Rumour was rife that Yves was upset, felt betrayed. Old loyalties lined up behind him. Merloz's career was finished before it started. Unless a miracle occurs to reinstate him, he has lost his chance of the big time. But, assuming that the press and opinion-makers had smiled on Merloz at his début show, how different it all could have been.

Lacroix's story is a warning to young designers and aspiring Bernard Arnaults alike. Arnault has found it difficult to live up to the media hype that greeted his designer's arrival on the scene. His firm has lost money consistently since it was founded in 1987. Even his own prophetically named perfume, C'est la vie!, packaged in the Provençal colours for which he had become known, is a loser, despite a launch party that stood all of Paris on its head and an ad budget in the region of $40 million. By 1988 the house of Lacroix had posted losses of $8 million, and the situation was to get worse. The bold prediction of Maurice Roger, chairman and chief executive officer of Parfums Christian Lacroix, that C'est la vie! would be the 'bestselling fragrance ever to hit the international market', looks rather silly now. The initial estimate of worldwide sales was quickly scaled down from $55 million to $36 million and it was downhill all the way from there. By 1991 US outlets for the scent were slashed from 600 to one. In February 1993 Louis Vuitton acquired Lacroix (minus perfume) for $14.5 million and, to date, the firm has recorded losses in excess of $36.4 million.

Inevitably, relations between creator and money men have soured. When Lacroix was asked by Paris *Interview* magazine if he ever felt like walking away from it all, he replied, 'Every day.' Although the remark was retracted – 'I was very tired and busy' – and things were patched up, it exposed the great stress under which designers have to function when things are not going well and they are effectively working for someone who does not necessarily understand them or their trade.

When the full history of the house of Lacroix is written it will become apparent that the designer was the victim of media hype from which it was extremely difficult to recover. Customers for his first few couture collections bought as a result of press pressure. The women who feel that they must wear the latest name came to Paris, read the reviews and bought. They then wondered what they had done. They did not understand the clothes; they did not know how to wear them. Most gave up and donated them to museums.

The Lacroix tale is a cautionary one. The formula for success was right. Each move seemed impeccable. So what went wrong? The timing. C'est la vie! appeared when Christian Lacroix's name was not sufficiently well known outside fashion circles to carry the scent. Fashion publicity is like a pool into which a stone bearing a designer's name has been dropped. The circles that ripple out-wards move comparatively slowly. The first circle involves the inside track – the people involved in the business or so obsessed with it that they *must* know what is going on. The second circle washes over the women who buy expensive clothing. The third takes in those who are generally interested in fashion and spend money on it but are far removed from 'designer' clothes and prices. The fourth circle includes the women who read magazines not primarily dedicated to fashion and shop in the middle-market stores. The fifth circle takes the name beyond fashion and into general currency. Few designers indeed reach that level. Most names stop at third- or fourth-wave level. Lacroix's scent was launched too early. His advisers believed their own publicity and became convinced that he was as big a name as they said. He was not. His name was still at second-circle level. In order to sell the vast quantities of scent required for success, a name requires true recognition and commitment on the High Street. It needs to be treated as a quantity commodity. How could Lacroix, known only for couture, with a label seen only in the most exclusive of boutiques and designer rooms, expect to command loyalty from the woman who goes to work by bus or subway? Such women buy Dior, YSL and Chanel, whose names have been made everyday items by vast publicity backed by huge promotional budgets. What they buy is not primarily a question of money. It is a question of identification. Ordinary women failed to identify with a man whom they saw as merely creating crazy clothes for self-indulgent jet-setters. And that is why Lacroix failed in the fragrance market. It is a failure, for all his loyal following at couture level and within the world's fashion press, that leaves a question mark over his future.

Like all major industries on a world scale, fashion has its Establishment. It includes the money men; the heads of some surprisingly large and extremely wealthy conglomerates, many of which were created in the last decade; and the leaders of old-established family firms, all of whom are driving the designer not merely to produce covetable clothes but to become a more marketable personality. Designers rely upon the press, PRs, retailers, socialites, advertisers and superstar personalities to help them become world figures. Many designers would probably be happy simply following their humble calling and creating beautiful clothes, but they are on a treadmill from which they cannot jump. As the costs of fashion escalate, the designer cannot be allowed not to be a personality because we, the public, cannot be relied upon to buy clothes if they do not come with the magic tag. The designer must frequently deny his integrity and bow to the values of the marketplace rather than those of the studio, in order to keep aloft a complex structure involving the livelihood of many thousands of people across the world. He must support the illusion that he is providing something that everyone not only *should* have, but *must* have.

There are plenty of informed fashion commentators convinced that the celebrity designer has no relevance to the Nineties and beyond. People want The Gap, J. C. Penney, Esprit, they argue. This may be true in a period of recession when traditional top-price designer markets such as Japan and Germany have temporarily collapsed, and name loyalty does not command the sales it once did, but it does not take into account the fact that the business of fashion needs top design input not merely for ideas but for many intangibles, not the least of which are glamour and probity.

As increasing amounts of money are required in order to make and maintain the big names, it is becoming obvious that a solution to present and future problems is to milk the top ones until they are dry. It has worked for Chanel, a house more successful now than it ever was in Coco's day. It has also worked with Christian Dior under Marc Bohan and, even more spectacularly, with Gianfranco Ferre as designer. It looks as if it might well work with de la Renta at Balmain.

Why should the house of Valentino stop when its eponymous head decides to retire? It does not make sense to allow huge business enterprises to disappear with the founder whose name they happen to bear. Galliano at Chloé; Marc Jacobs for Donna Karan; Isaac Mizrahi at Geoffrey Beene; Rifat Ozbek for Bill Blass? All would be quite acceptable in an industry where the name is everything. Take this a stage forward. Maybe there won't be any more great names. Perhaps we do not need them. There is, after all, only one conspicuous gap in the present celebrity line-up. There should – and must, eventually – be a major black designer. Then there would be every reason to maintain the status quo and infiltrate the new talent into existing design houses.

There should be no more disappointments like Lacroix, no sad waste of talent as with Merloz. Young designers would be able to exploit their skills and reach their potential within the safe carapace of a name known for success, a name that cannot be allowed to fail. The house of Worth lasted for a hundred years. Why should it not happen again?

Before Arnault tempted him away, Lacroix had done wonders in bringing prominence back to the house of Patou. Indeed, at the height of the business flurry of the 1980s it seemed that all that was required for a magic carpet ride was the marriage of an old and respected name in couture – the name of a designer, long dead – and a currently successful ready-to-wear designer with 'profile'.

The most convincing of couture marriages – and the one that has lasted most successfully – is that between the house of Chanel and Karl Lagerfeld. It is a liaison that has brought dazzling financial success. But not everyone in Paris is totally happy with what Lagerfeld has done with the Chanel fashion philosophy. Many claim that he is dancing on the grave of Coco Chanel's feminist beliefs and trampling underfoot her strongly held views on the need for logic in clothing.

But it is not enough to buy a signature. What happened at Lanvin chilled *tout* Paris as thoroughly as Lacroix's doings at Patou had elated it. Lanvin surprised everyone in the late 1980s by appointing Claude Montana – a highly respected cult figure in ready-to-wear – to design its couture range. Montana tried to be as rational in couture as Lacroix had been irrational. He set out to make clothes with which modern women could empathise, clothes they might actually wish to wear. His endeavours were misunderstood. Because many people wished to preserve the mystique of couture, the clothes were judged a resounding flop. Montana took the lesson to heart and his next collection was a brilliant piece of tightrope-walking. It maintained the discipline of line for which he is famous while being sufficiently luxurious to fit the perceived notion of what couture should be. Nevertheless, the Montana–Lanvin cooperation did not last, and the whole episode put a brake on couture euphoria. What was realised by the shrewder heads in Paris was that modernising a great name from couture's past only works if it is fantasised at the same time.

5

Family Feuds

One of the enduring myths that supports the designer scam is that you get what you pay for. It suggests that the maestro whose name adorns the label has not only created the garment, but has taken responsibility for its manufacture, and for its quality control. While it is true that he may have been responsible for the design, and will probably have approved it even if it was created by an unnamed assistant, the manufacturing side of fashion is its own world, far from that of the couturiers' salons. Even if the labels on the clothes represent designers with widely different approaches to dress, the garments are likely to have been made by the same people in the same factory, working for a firm completely unknown to the average customer.

If people think of anything – apart from the bill – when they buy designer fashion – an Armani jacket or a Versace suit, for example – it is probably the workmanship that has gone into such a highly crafted garment. They assume that Armani and Versace and all the great ready-to-wear designers have their own factories to produce their range under the guidance and control of the maestro. They convince themselves that they are paying for quality as well as the exclusivity of the designer's point of view. To a certain degree, they are right. Quality control of top-label brands is an important investment in the future for a designer. If it is neglected, even the grandest name will lose its lustre.

Designers work on such a varied scale that they simply cannot afford to run their own factories. They farm out the production of their clothes to industrial entrepreneurs who make them, promise quality and ensure that they are delivered at the time agreed by the designer and the retail outlets. This being said, only a foolish designer would abdicate all responsibility for clothes that will bear his label. The top brands are normally monitored to ensure that they are made as well as they are designed, although I have seen designer label clothes in famous stores and boutiques with loose threads, buttons about to come off and even sleeves sewn in back-to-front.

The right to produce designer ranges is hotly fought over. Top manufacturers, riding on the boom in top labels, paid handsomely in the Eighties for the big names. They invested huge amounts of capital in plant, machinery, distribution services and highly sophisticated computer technology in order to beat the opposition and woo the best names. Their reward was vast profits. The Steilman group in Germany, maker of the Karl Lagerfeld signature ranges and over twenty other collections, had an amazing decade and, even when sales slumped in the 1990s, was still able to command annual revenues in excess of a billion dollars. But the giants who captured the blue-chip designer names were mostly Italian. The Marzotto group, the Miroglio group and, most prestigious of all, Gruppo GFT, made the advertising myth that equated 'Made in Italy' with top quality, a reality that also attracted designers from France and the US.

Gruppo Marzotto, 60 per cent owned by the Marzotto family who founded it in 1836, had a revenue in 1992 of $1.583 billion. Since its acquisition of Hugo Boss in 1991 it has been Europe's largest producer of men's tailored garments. It manufactures for Gianfranco Ferre, Enrico Coveri and Laura Biagotti, as well as making four lines for Missoni. It is one of Europe's leading producers of linen thread and pure wool fabric, with distribution of textiles and apparel to over eighty countries.

In 1992, when Gruppo GFT – the world's largest designer-label manufacturer – ran into financial trouble, the Rivetti family which owned the company (Maurizio Rivetti, the chairman, his brother and two sisters holding 25 per cent of the shares each) turned to Marzotto with ideas of a merger. They were also rumoured to be in talks with Benetton who were said to be looking for a way of taking their world-famous name upmarket. Gruppo GFT was losing money heavily – almost $12 million in the first half of 1992 – but it was still a very attractive possibility for any company looking to expand *and* gain prestige.

Gruppo GFT was manufacturer for the 'famous four' – Armani, Valentino, Claude Montana and Emanuel Ungaro – as well as making clothes for Ralph Lauren's Polo, Pierre Cardin, Christian Dior and Calvin Klein, and lines such as Stone Island. It owned 43 controlled or affiliated companies and 16 production units in Europe, Asia and America. Even with financial problems, its 1992 revenue was $1.2 billion, putting it eighth in the fashion magazine *W Fashion Europe*'s Top 100. But the 'famous four' were the jewel in Gruppo GFT's crown. The two Armani lines had 1992 sales of over $177 million; the eight Valentino lines chalked up $155 million; Montana's two lines brought in almost $23 million, and Ungaro's five lines added just under $89 million.

Nothing came of the talks with Marzotto or Benetton, but Gruppo Tessile Miroglio SpA, ten in *W*'s ranking, bought a 50 per cent stake in GFT early in 1993 for a figure in the region of $1.7 billion. Together, the merged firm created a giant that would bestraddle the world, with aggregate sales in the region of $2.11 billion.

Gruppo Miroglio, yet another wholly owned family firm, already had 43 companies, 31 of which were outside Italy, and its 30 production plants – spread across Europe, North Africa and Egypt – employed 6,200 people. But it had little experience of designer apparel, only producing clothes at that level for Krizia (the Per Te line), Daniel Hechter and its own line, Rubino, created by Byblos designers Keith Varty and Alan Cleaver. Even during negotiations, fundamental differences in the philosophy and attitudes of Miroglio and GFT became apparent. Further, designers happy with GFT were less so with the new con- glomerate. They feared a drop in standards, quoting Miroglio's limited experience in manufacturing designer clothes and Carlo Miroglio's well known lack of sympathy for designer airs and graces. There seemed a strong possibility that many GFT designers would renege. Instead, it was Miroglio who backed out, leaving the Rivetti company high and dry in July 1993, just as GFT Donna had announced the launch of its own-line medium-priced women's range, Sahza, which hoped to capitalise on post-recession price- conscious customers who wanted quality, but not at any cost.

The troubles at GFT, which seem to have been solved by bringing in Clemente Signoroni from Fiat as managing director, show clearly how totally the days of 'buy anything, pay anything' Eighties' euphoria have gone. GFT has too many luxury designer names on its books and they have been the most vulnerable to recession, with dramatic drops in sales across the world. They also mark the demise, at least temporarily, of the 'Italian Miracle', which seemed such a permanent part of the fashion scene throughout the 1980s. Italian fashion in the past fifteen years became strong in the world because it had a solid base at home. The best customers for 'Made in Italy' were the Italians. Boutiques throughout the country, from Bari to Bergamo, were thriving outlets for designer fashion. But by mid-1993 thousands of them had failed and at least as many again were feeling the pinch. In 1992, 160,000 textile and apparel industry jobs were lost across the EC. May 1993 saw a record 8,000 companies, including a high percentage of fashion firms, fail in France. Italian garment produc- tion dropped by 9 per cent in the first six months of 1993 and Paolo Marzotto was predicting a 20 per cent drop in menswear sales for the whole year.

In addition, the Italian Miracle suffered from the exposure of corruption in Italy and the Mani Pulite (clean hands) campaign that swept the country, making 'kick-back' money harder to come by. Even those who still managed to get kick-backs wanted to keep quiet about it. No more flaunting. No more excess. No more designer clothes. And it slowly became apparent that much of the Italian miracle had been based on the circulation of money. Vast bribes and 'considerations', costing Italy a reputed $6 billion annually, had given the middle classes unprecedented amounts of uncommitted funds that it was in everybody's interest to keep moving. What better way of ensuring the currency's buoyancy than by investing in designer clothing? The collapse of Italy will have repercussions that will rumble on for years, but it is already clear that the luxury garment industry will be one of the areas hardest hit. It is a fact already acknowledged by the determination of top Italian designers to push into North America – the only market with even the slightest claim to liveliness in the 1990s – with renewed vigour in order to counteract losses on the home front and take advantage of the exchange rate, with the lira showing a 30 per cent drop against the dollar. The intriguing question remains: with fewer boutiques and, perhaps, fewer labels, will the Italians lose their lead as the world's *numero uno* fashion-conscious country? And, if interest wanes along with sales, what will happen to all the country's fashion magazines? Will some of them become redundant too?

When the going gets tough, the tough get touchy. Internecine strife and family quarrels grow as markets shrink. The Italian firm Gruppo Genny SpA, owners of Byblos, ran into trouble in 1993 with Keith Varty and Alan Cleaver no longer working exclusively for the Byblos line, Gianni Versace severing connections with the Genny label, for which he had been consultant for many years, and, most dramatic of all, Donatella Girombelli, wife of founder Arnaldo Girombelli who died in 1983, ousting her brother-in-law

Sergio Girombelli from the presidency of Byblos, a post he had held for ten years. Genny, owned by the Girombelli family, with Donatella holding 38 per cent, was in the throes of civil war. Sergio was replaced as chairman by Valleriano Balloni, professor of economics at Ancona University, home town of Genny; presumably it is hoped that his appointment will reverse the 12 per cent drop in revenue that marked 1992 trading.

Genny is an upmarket firm with a strong design content. In addition to Versace and Varty and Cleaver, its Complice line is designed by Italy's most successful team, Dolce & Gabbana. Its products are international and highly sophisticated. The fact that such a firm is in trouble spells out how badly companies are faring in the first half of the 1990s. But family quarrels and industrial problems strike at all levels. Betrayals, deceits, quarrels are all part of the international fashion scene. And it is no surprise to anyone that they appear most often in Italy, where firms tend to keep everything in the family.

Italy has more successful family businesses than any other country in the world. The seven Fendi sisters sit astride a multinational handbag, furs and accessories empire worth over $100 million in annual sales. The Ferragamo family presides over a footwear and accessories company worth almost $200 million in revenue. The sports and knitwear firm of Stefanel, worth $380 million, is 65 per cent owned by the Stefanel family. Max Mara, a group which, in addition to the eponymous line, includes Sportmax and Marina Rinaldi and has a revenue of $795 million, is wholly owned by the Maramotti family. Benetton, second only to Financière Agache and Coats Viyella, owners of Jaeger, Van Heusen and Viyella, in the cavalcade of Europe's fashion industry, is 79.9 per cent family owned.

Under the leadership of its chairman Luciano Benetton, the firm has frequently generated controversy – not least for its advertising campaigns – but United Colors of Benetton now has 14 factories and more than 7,000 retail stores in over 100 countries around the world. Famous as Benetton is, it is the company's other line, Sisley, that is largely responsible for the group's annual revenue of more than $2 billion and the fact that Benetton has been the fastest grower among all group bands over the past three years. Fashion accounts for 99 per cent of Benetton's revenue, as opposed to Agache, where it makes up only a quarter of the total business. Benetton is a proven success as a *fashion* firm, relying virtually entirely on clothes for its income.

Family quarrels are rife in Italian fashion. Those of the Gucci family in the early 1980s electrified the fashion world for years. Not without their comic aspect, they included personal rifts and accusations, physical fights in the boardroom and a $13 million lawsuit. Final winner in the protracted battle for power was Maurizio Gucci, who consolidated his position by reorganising the company and bringing in Dawn Mello, ex-president of Bergdorf's, in 1989 as senior vice-president and image director. It says much for the growing power of the American consumer and the need for US sales that a job which, only ten years ago, could not conceivably have been done by a non-Italian, was given to a member of the nation traditionally felt in Italy to have little to offer Europe, apart from consumer dollars.

Gucci brought in Mello because, while all the internecine squabbles had been taking place, something had happened to the Gucci name in the marketplace. From being a 'must have' for fashion sophisticates, Gucci merchandise had become, if not exactly vulgar, something not quite right for cool young fashion followers. The Gucci image had been fatally weakened by the Japanese, who went overboard for it to such a degree in the Seventies that the via Condotti flagship shop in Rome had long queues forming daily at its door – a door which frequently had to be kept closed in order to keep out the crowds of tourists, hell bent on purchase of *anything* Gucci, in case they prevented those already inside from doing the same. Something in the Gucci image had slipped; it had become a fashion insider's joke. Dawn Mello's job was to rescue it.

She did so by slashing the number of Gucci products by half – from 10,000 to 5,000. In their place, Mello re-established Gucci classics that she found in the old pattern books and archives going back to the early days of the firm, which was founded in 1922. Her efforts were praised by the press, but Gucci revenue was rumoured to have dropped by a staggering $20 million in 1992. Maurizio Gucci maintained that the firm's problems were merely a hiccup, unavoidable when a company is undergoing a massive internal restructuring programme, but others were not totally convinced. One of the sceptics was Maurizio Gucci's co-shareholder, the Bahrain-based Investcorp. Although they owned 50 per cent of the shares, Maurizio Gucci's 50 per cent had the added advantage that he had management control. As Gucci denied financial troubles and dismissed tales of increasingly embattled relationships with Investcorp, informed observers prepared to watch a fight to the death over control of the company.

Any businessman who deals with Italian firms knows that there is often more than one set of books for a company. Three is the most common number: one to show to fiscal authorities, one for the partners and one for the family. It is not difficult to imagine which, if any, gives a true picture of a firm's financial situation. *Women's Wear Daily* reported that rumours suggested Gucci losses of over $30 million in 1991, even though the firm maintained that the company had broken even at that time. In a deepening crisis over mutual trust in May 1993, Gucci, under pressure to settle a creditor judgement, found the money at the last moment and told Investcorp, as reported in *WWD*, that 'after being visited in a dream by the ghost of his father, he found the money to pay the multi-million-dollar debt, hidden under the floor of his home in St Moritz'. Gucci laughed at their gullibility and said the story was his 'nice, Italian way' of telling Investcorp to mind their own business.

The battle appears to be over. Maurizio Gucci has relinquished control of the firm in favour of Investcorp, who paid over $100 million to gain control. After seventy years, there is no longer a Gucci at Gucci.

The essentials of the Gucci story have been played out several times since the end of the 1980s, with revered and apparently well-established names suddenly finding themselves in trouble. It is a scenario that is not confined to Italy. Both Lanvin and Balmain in Paris have had their problems in the last couple of years. The turbulent times at Lanvin began in 1990 when L'Oréal and Louis Vuitton bought the house from Midland Bank for FF 500 million. Company president Michel Pietrini, hired from Chanel where his revitalising policies – including hiring Karl Lagerfeld as a designer – had been highly successful, decided that the Lanvin image was incoherent, mainly because there were too many designers all following disparate lines. He conceived a Grand Plan which would include scrapping many licences, regaining control of Lanvin output and projecting a modern, controlled image. One of the problems with many of the famous fashion and beauty firms is that internal politics bubble away and the man in charge is allowed to play with them to his heart's content – until he fails. Lanvin clearly had its problems, but they were not helped by Pietrini's personality, which manifested itself in decisions such as his dramatic sacking of Claude Montana, the company's couture designer, in January 1992, on the day of his highly successful second show. Paris was shocked at the timing but could understand Pietrini's decision: Montana's earlier attempts to modernise Lanvin couture had not been an unqualified success with customers or press.

It was Pietrini's choice of replacement that made Paris wonder about his judgement. In an interview that lasted no more than five minutes, Pietrini offered the post of ready-to-wear and accessories designer to Dominique Morlotti, ex-menswear designer at Christian Dior who, although he admits he 'was not expecting that . . . said "yes" right away'. The fashion world was as stunned as Morlotti. His only experience of womenswear was a brief seven months with minor designer Popy Moreni. Gossip in Paris suggested that he had designed menswear at Dior on computers and had no real experience of fitting or cutting women's garments. Pietrini sailed serenely forward, embarking on an expensive crusade to buy back control of the Lanvin retail network and revamping the firm's flagship boutiques for men and women in Faubourg St-Honoré. Designed by Conran Associates as the last word in prestige premises, they could have helped turn round Lanvin fortunes even though the grandeur of scale and appoint-ments meant that they cost Lanvin over FF 100 million, but the Gulf War and the slump meant that trade was slow. Lanvin lost FF 130 million in 1992 and nobody was surprised when Pietrini's place was taken in April 1993 by Loic Armand, a reliable L'Oréal man who had been in charge of one of the firm's subsidiaries in Mexico.

It would seem that company chairmen and chief executive officers cannot bear to leave things alone. The moment they snatch the ball, they feel the they must run with it – somewhere . . . anywhere. They have an almost paranoid compulsion to make their mark. The case of Alain Chevalier at Balmain – where Pietrini's Marlotti had worked briefly – illustrates the problems only too well. When Chevalier left his job as chairman of LVMH in 1989, he bought the house of Balmain from its Canadian owner, Erich Fayer.

In terms of ready-to-wear and couture, the house of Balmain had become a non-event in the years after the death of Pierre Balmain in 1982. But it had a useful clutch of licensees – especially in Japan – and a scent, Ivoire, which sold reasonably well. Its potential was limited but at least it *had* potential. Chevalier was considered sound, and was generally credited as the mastermind behind the Louis Vuitton/Moët-Hennessy merger, the man who made Parfums Christian Dior a world force. This won him backing from the Peugeot family holding company, Société Foncière, and banks of the standing of Société Général and Crédit Agricole. With their help, he paid Fayer FF 550 million for Balmain.

The sum surprised Paris. Balmain was a house struggling to keep going on sales of a mere FF 160 million a year. Nevertheless, Chevalier vigorously addressed what he considered to be the problems and needs of his new company. Erik Mortensen, who had been Balmain's assistant and had carried on designing after his death, left the firm. Chevalier, ignoring the fact that Ivoire had made FF 54 million in 1989, decided to revive the fortunes of another Balmain fragrance, Vent Vert, which in comparison had made a mere FF 1 million in the same period. Despite the FF 40 million that was spent on rebuilding the Balmain fragrance empire, revenue fell to a mere FF 47 million in 1990. In the meantime, Chevalier had appointed Alastair Blair as ready-to-wear designer and Hervé Pierre for couture. Then, to everyone's surprise, Chevalier announced that Balmain would no longer have a couture line. There was uproar from the licensees, especially those in Japan who made up a fifth of the Balmain revenue. The yelps of horror were so great that Chevalier was forced to go, cap in hand, to the controlling body of French couture, the Chambre Syndicale, and ask for a dispensation whereby his firm could be taken back into couture although it was unable to produce the statutory number of outfits necessary for membership.

By the end of his first year at Balmain, Chevalier had run up losses of FF 90.8 million on sales of only FF 138 million. The banks panicked and tried to sell over Chevalier's head. The Société Foncière wrote off FF 70 million. Balmain was sold back to its previous owner, Erich Fayer, in June 1991 for FF 100 million. Fayer was the only man involved who did not get his fingers burned.

What went wrong? Like Pietrini, Chevalier attempted to do too much too quickly and, inevitably, his plans were badly affected by the slump. The general opinion in Paris was that he had paid far too much for Balmain in the first place, an error that would have weakened any chance of eventual success, even if Chevalier had not made such a mess of the perfume side of the business. Instead of spending money on Vent Vert, Chevalier would have been wiser to build on the success of Ivoire and go forward with that as a base for future profits.

Many in Paris believe that Chevalier was given an impossible task in that he was allowed only eighteen months for a job requiring at least six years. They feel that he was badly served by the banks who, instead of biting the bullet and continuing to fund Balmain on a long-term footing, lost their nerve and pulled the plug. Pierre Bergé commented, 'When a house is breathless, mouth-to-mouth resuscitation won't revive it. . . . You must have imagination and creativity.' Although money is clearly important in these circumstances, it represents only one side of a rescue equation. Flair, courage and foresight are also vital to success.

Judgement is the most crucial thing of all. Too little investment can sink a firm's growth at a critical moment but, if the basic philosophy of a company is not right, no amount of money can save it. One of the greatest dangers is over-expansion at the wrong moment and this has affected many in the cross-winds from 1980s buoyancy to 1990s insecurity. Even a firm like the German ready-to-wear business, Escada, has been caught on the hop by changed circumstances, although its product appears to be as popular as ever. Founded in 1979 by Margaretha and Wolfgang Ley, it was one of the great success stories of the Eighties. The firm, named after a racehorse, was, in Margaretha Ley's words, 'Creating clothes for working women with a certain amount of money'. The target customer was a businesswoman who wanted sophisticated but colourful clothes for her working and social life. Margaretha Ley was the right woman to give it to them, having learned the designer's trade at Jacques Fath in Paris and with the German ready-to-wear firm of Mondi. Her husband Wolfgang was a businessman, but he was *au fait* with all areas of fashion.

Margaretha Ley died of cancer in June 1992, aged 56. She left a strong and well-trained design team at Escada, a firm that had gone public in Germany in 1986, but in which the Leys retained a 51 per cent stake. Although sales in 1991 had reached $85 million, they represented a drop in pre-tax profits of 24 per cent. In November 1992 the firm recorded its first ever losses – due, according to informed sources, to an attempt to expand too quickly, without consolidating gains. *Women's Wear Daily* described the Escada pace of expansion as 'blistering'. Between 1981 and 1990 the Leys set up eight foreign distribution companies and bought four apparel companies. By the beginning of 1993, Escada was expecting losses of $61 million and put up a subsidiary – St John Knits – for sale at $100 million to cover the debt and a 30 per cent plunge in the value of Escada stock.

Recession presented foreign exchange problems to international firms but, above all, as Wolfgang Ley has said, the real body blow was that all the major markets collapsed at the same time: Japan, America and Europe, including Germany, are all suffering. This is the one thing that even the most pessimistic or shrewd financial forecasters did not dare to contemplate. But the unthinkable happened.

For many sections of the fashion industry it has been a disaster, but for the public it could well act as a cleansing fire. Economic hardship has bitten deep into the designer scam. With money short, consumers are not so easily gulled as they are when it can be spent without much thought. Firms like Escada, whose products have proven worth, will survive, as will most of the top designers. What is more likely to disappear on the tidal wave of economic hardship is the hyped price scale of good-class clothing and the lack of concern over quality and value for money that characterised the excesses of the 1980s.

6

Sweet Smell of Excess

The 1980s were unprecedented in the way major retail stores chased designer names, determined to sell their clothes and prepared to accept all sorts of conditions, provisos and restraints. Designers demanded their own sales areas, instore shops, special promotions and displays, and were given them. Designers were also busy opening their own boutiques, frequently more than one per city. There was no sense of overkill, no premonition of how so many outlets would survive if a blip appeared on the economic scene. Why should there be? Customers were flocking in. They couldn't buy enough. Balance sheets continued to shine rosily and everyone smiled. Surely the good times would roll for ever.

They did not. Now everyone is much more cautious and designers especially are determined not to spread their names too thinly. Like everyone else in fashion, they are desperately looking for new ways to keep the lucrative designer scam alive – if only ticking over – until things improve. Forward-looking businessmen are thinking revolution: they fear that the gravy train of the *ancien régime* is over for this century, and maybe even longer. The search for new outlets is on.

Nothing shows the revolution that is taking place in fashion retail, and the pressures on traditional methods of selling, as clearly as the Battle for Barneys. The stores that count in Manhattan – Bloomingdale's, Bergdorf Goodman, Macy's and Saks Fifth Avenue – are in uptown, East Side locations. The exception is Barneys, situated on Seventh Avenue and 17th Street in Chelsea.

For years little more than a discount store, Barneys went upmarket with a vengeance in the Eighties, carrying the very best of established fashion lines and avant-garde young designers. But, for many New Yorkers – and more tourists – the location was still a problem. The logical outcome of the upmarket move was a literal move uptown. A second Barneys was created on the hallowed Upper East Side, at Madison Avenue and East 61st Street. Eager buyers for the store turned to their designers, anxious to show just how advantageous the new store would prove for them.

They were in for a shock. Top companies who in the 1980s would have been delighted to have another Manhattan outlet had looked at their balance sheets in the 1990s and decided that enough was enough. When there is too much competition, they decided, it makes no sense to create more. The Battle for Barneys began with Chanel refusing to sell to the new store because it was too near to its own boutique, scheduled for expansion, on East 57th Street. Other designer companies began to assess the position of their own sites and to notice how close Barneys uptown would be to the other large stores who, equally aware of the problem, had begun to squeeze designers with contract stipulations, 'carrots' over guarantees and space allocation, and promises of deals on advertising, window space and special promotions. Chanel was joined by other refusees, including Ralph Lauren. Karl Lagerfeld said, 'It does not help business to open an account with a competitor next door. We cannot add a fourth door uptown.' Pierre Bergé, the contumacious head of Yves Saint Laurent, refused Rive Gauche to the store because, according to him, Barneys had reneged on a promised special area for YSL perfumes. Once they knew that they had lost Rive Gauche, Barneys returned the Merloz collection they had bought as part of the deal. This was a calculated act of aggression, and Bergé did not take kindly to seeing his latest young protégé scorned after a launch reputedly costing $4 million of YSL money.

Acrimony increased dramatically when Giorgio Armani decided not to sell to Barneys for its new location. The store, which was already being described as 'the time bomb gone uptown', unearthed a clause in a 1979 contract with Armani which said that any disputes had to go to international arbitration. Wriggle as they might – and they did, by arguing that company and store were so transformed that a ruling of fourteen years earlier could have no meaning in 1993 – Armani had to submit to arbitration and a court in Geneva found in favour of Barneys, ordering Armani to sell to both Barneys stores in New York. Most designers sided with Armani, who pointed out that in 1979 his company was unknown in America and Barneys was still a single-unit men's store. Establishment opinion hardened against the store, which was left to beat the bushes for less prestigious names who were neither committed to other stores nor grand enough to have their own boutiques. It did so very successfully. In the first five days after its opening in September 1993, Barneys – the biggest speciality store to open in Manhattan since Bergdorf Goodman on Fifth Avenue in 1929 – chalked up sales of $6 million.

Frightened designers no longer dare risk having too many outlets because they know this merely increases the opportunity for their precious, prestigious labels to be put on sale at damaging reductions. And not even a store with the impeccable designer-label profile of a Barneys could budge them – although good sales figures might eventually persuade where argument failed.

Designers are under pressure in the new retail situation created by the slump. Sales of new signature ranges began to slacken off even in the 'pay and display' 1980s and they are still slipping. In 1992 sales of ready-to-wear labels from the 21 couturiers and 25 other members of the French Chambre Syndicale dropped by 5 per cent, registering at $1.01 billion. In Italy, textile and clothing exports dropped by 5 per cent in 1991, the worst figures since 1980. After disastrous figures for 1991, the prestigious Comité Colbert group of French luxury firms, which includes in its 73 members Chanel, Dior, Givenchy, Hermès and Louis Vuitton, showed an increase in 1992 of 2.45 per cent with sales totalling $5.27 billion – but only after the French government had cut tax on luxury goods, including furs, perfume and jewellery, by 3.4 per cent. In an effort to promote Italian fashion, the Italian Trade Commission in New York spent $12 million of government money in 1992 on a special 'Discovery of Italy' promotion.

The designers' answer to the problem has changed the nature of fashion shopping. Increasingly, it is becoming hard to find a designer shop that devotes even a quarter of its selling and display space to the main-line collections. Companies have turned to diffusion or secondary lines which deliberately avoid design originality and novelty for bread-and-butter wearability at a more affordable price, but still with the cachet of the designer's name: they are sold in less exclusive outlets, with a price tag about 30 per cent lower than that of the signature range.

This development has led to a certain monotony in the fashion world. There is not even all that much difference in style between many designers, particularly in the secondary lines: it requires a sophisticated eye to know whether a jacket is by Blass, YSL, de la Renta or Ferre. The difference often is apparent only to the expert. Of course, the designer's *major* jacket statement of any year, highlighted on the runway and photographed for the fashion magazines, is much more easily spotted – but for every one of those that is for sale, there will be hundreds of less original, less demanding jackets which can be worn for several seasons to come.

The whiz-bang fun of the show has less and less connection with what is available at the sales point as the world economy continues to limp. The cost of originality in lost sales is too great a risk to take. Even Giorgio Armani, who has always eschewed catwalk fire-works and has consistently built his shows on clothes which would be put up for sale with little alteration or adaptation, finds that his Black Label full-strength collection is too expensive for most women. He has been obliged to introduce secondary ranges, including the phenomenally successful A/X line, geared specifically to North America.

Secondary lines are, however, seen most strongly in Italy, and have been a vibrant money-spinner on the Milan fashion scene for the past ten years: Emporio by Armani; Oliver by Valentino, which netted retail sales of $42 million in 1991; Miss V – again by Valentino – a line begun in 1972; Oaks by Ferre, going back to 1978 and joined in 1988 by 000.1 Ferre; Moschino's Cheap and Cheerful, which accounted for 26 per cent of the $163 million Moschino turnover for 1991; Versace's Instante (from 1988), Versus (1990), and V2 by Versace (1991), which, along with Versace Jeans, accounts for $194.8 million that the designer makes from secondary lines.

Designers famous to the public for rich embroidery and beading; designers who experiment with shapes and scale; designers, in short, who capture the headlines each season, all know that their money will be made not by extravagant show-stoppers, but by the basics – an all-purpose jacket, a flattering skirt, an adaptable blouse and well-cut pants. Everything else is literally showbiz. But, of course, they do not wish to be known for such banal items. That is why they continue to create memorable looks for the show. They also know that they need them for publicity, because these are the clothes that magazine editors crave. How many women would buy *Vogue* if its pages were full of basic wardrobe items and nothing else? Reading a glossy fashion magazine is for many women an escapist experience. Kill that element and they will not bother to read it at all. But it is not just magazine editors who need the outfit that will capture the imagination of the reader. The designer does, too. The woman excited by the glamour of his show clothes will want to buy a little piece of that glamour when she goes looking for an 'everyday' jacket and will choose the one that carries his label.

The glamour of the secondary lines and the shops that sell them is hyped to an extraordinary extent. An opening or launch must be original enough and sufficiently 'different' to attract attention and get customers inside shops. At times, promotional gimmicks can seem desperate; the launch of Armani A/X Exchange in America in 1992 took place at several stores simultaneously in an effort to make an impact. Saks, Neiman Marcus and Bloomingdale's sent customers a gift of nuts and bolts – symbol of the new range which was meant to be about no-nonsense, no-frills, straightforward and practical clothing – which they could exchange at the store for an A/X T-shirt or baseball cap. It was a cute idea which worked – backed by the impact of forty Bloomingdale's windows devoted to A/X Exchange and special A/X walkways through the store to guide the eager customer to the merchandise. When Henri Bendel opened a 540-square-feet store area exclusively for Claude Montana they created a special entrance for it, devoted all their Fifth Avenue windows to Montana and flew in their best customers for the event.

There are other strategies for promoting sales in a depressed market. US designer Bill Blass is the frontrunner of an approach that is changing the nature of fashion retailing and fashion shows in the States.

Blass is the darling of the ladies who lunch. Handsome, rich and unattached, he is New York's undisputed 'walker' designer now that his only real rival, Oscar de la Renta, has remarried. But Blass is also the darling of chief executive officers of major retail stores across America – a group much less easily charmed – because he is a proven seller on the increasingly important trunk show circuit. He has done these shows for years, ever since his early realisation that 'to be a successful designer you can't stay in New York . . . I went on the road to places like Dallas and Detroit and found out what women really wanted .'

And what women in America want is a share of that Le Cirque

and Le Grenouille chic that Bill's New York socialite ladies have in such abundance. That is why Bill Blass never deems time spent at a charity bash, society dinner or art opening as time wasted. Always squiring a high-profile lady of fashion, he partakes of the aura of her international reputation. It rubs off on him and his clothes. This is how women like Judy Peabody, Susan Gutfreund and Lynn Wyatt play a small but real role in the dissemination of fashion. They are read about in every city in the States and, when Bill comes to town with his frocks, they are remembered. Women flock to his trunk shows not merely to buy clothes but also to buy into something much more important: the glamour of international sophistication that by association Bill brings to their own down-town store.

To be fair to Blass, they would probably come anyway. He has a devastating charm that completely enraptured Diana Vreeland and ensured that he was a regular diner at the White House in the days of the Reagan administration. But he works hard at it, nevertheless, and the trunk show is one of his most important outlets. With the true buccaneering spirit of merchandising that characterises the history of North American retailing – 'If folks can't come to you, take it to them!' – he puts on between ninety and a hundred shows a year in places as diverse as Tallahassee and Tampico. Of these, he will make a personal appearance at, perhaps, eight of the more prestigious stores in a season, whilst a highly trained sales force looks after the rest. Slick and professional, they can slip customers into clothes that they will find irresistible as adroitly as they can whiz their credit cards through the cash register.

Since the Eighties' bonanza in designer signature labels slumped, the extra push given by trunk shows has become more popular than ever with designers and with stores. As the president of Carolina Herrera's company has pointed out, anything with a price tag over $2,500 requires a special sales effort that only a trunk show can produce. Stores simply can't take the risk of stocking such merchandise in a climate of recession. And that is one of the greatest attractions of the trunk show: it enables the customer to see the designer's complete range, properly shown and fully accessorised. Showing the entire collection invariably generates multiple purchases as customers choose shoes and accessories to go with their major selections. The whole experience is subtly engineered to give the customer a feeling of privilege and the sort of personal consideration that she used to get in the old days, with consultations with the *vendeuse* and time spent in fittings, which were once part of buying major wardrobe items each season from an exclusive store.

Things are different now. Trunk shows take place early in the morning – often before store opening hours – and invitations are for the favoured few. These are the fifty to one hundred private customers who wish to meet the designer over breakfast – coffee, croissants and counselling – see the video of the show or a live presentation, and then buy. And they really do buy. De la Renta, who personally attends about ten shows out of a hundred in a season, has his own sales staff for these occasions. He normally mounts a two-day event, and expects to clock up sales of at least $100,000. Donna Karan, with six regionally based sales teams, has about fifty shows a season and they bring in about $13 million annually. She expects an event at a major store to produce sales of between $100,000 and $200,000 and, for 'B' doors (less important stores) between $50,000 and $75,000.

Sales are highest when the designer is present but, if the name is big enough, figures can shoot up even if he is not. This is especially true of European designers. In a two-day event at Saks Fifth Avenue for Giorgio Armani's top-price Black Label collection, sales reached $750,000, including thirty-four striped pant suits at $3,000 each. A two-day Chanel show at Bloomingdale's, initiated by a private show of the collection for fifty customers, resulted in sales of $675,00. Quilted leather pants at $3,000 and leather blazers at $3,600 sold out. No wonder Blass increased his trunk shows by 30 per cent in 1992. They accounted for almost half of his $10 million signature collection business.

And this is the great value of a trunk show. Highly trained people – acting as old-style saleswomen did in the 1950s – cajole and flatter customers into buying the designer's top-of-the-range label. And it works because the customer *is* flattered by the attention, wowed by the glamour of the designer's presence and thrilled by the sense of specialness which is carefully built into the whole experience.

But the fight for the market means that designers and retailers must try harder at all levels. Extravagance is the name of the game when it comes to raising product consciousness in fashion. It does not merely mean spending money; it is equally about imagination, style and wit. Above all, perhaps, it is about attention to detail. All designers insist that everything is checked and controlled by themselves or a trusted senior member of their staff before any move is made or any member of the public gets near a newly opened boutique or salesroom.

Another change to the retail scene may come from a breeze, not as yet a wind, that is blowing ever stronger in North America and might well become a force in Britain before the century is out. It threatens to alter the nature of retailing more profoundly than any development in the last century. TV selling of fashion and luxury goods has been slow in coming but, in the last two years in America, has been attracting a new level of commitment by some of the country's top retail outlets.

Sharp magazine publishers are already taking on board the possibilities offered by television shopping – which has been around in America for almost ten years but has not, until recently, been seen as a quality outlet to be taken seriously. All of that changed when entrepreneur Barry Diller, ex-head of the Fox movie and TV empire, paid $25 million for a 3 per cent stake in QVC which, along with the Home Shopping Network (HSN), was the only survivor from the twenty or so US TV shopping networks of the mid-1980s. QVC and HSN offer 24-hour-a-day, 7-day-a-week shopping and, together, pull in about $2 billion in sales per year. Designers know that an appearance on TV can already net them sales of up to $1 million.

Interactive TV, whereby viewers can order fashion merchandise via their remote control, allows US viewers, through cable TV, to receive as many as 500 channels and is expected to have a huge impact on retailing in North America. It has already proved that it can initiate as well as promote fashion. MTV, the pioneering cable music station seen in 55 million US households and 220 million worldwide, has, since its inception, been a useful selling tool for fashion. Veejays – who are on air an average of 300 times a year – create a huge demand for clothes to wear. The show borrows them from designers and always credits them when first worn. Some designers are nervous about the downmarket appeal of the show and won't lend. Prominent refusers are Isaac Mizrahi, Yohji Yamamoto and Comme des Garçons, but the showbiz kids such as Versace or Gaultier are only too happy to oblige, as are Dolce & Gabbana, Levis, Moschino Jeans and Todd Oldham. But in 1992 MTV moved things forward for their own good and launched a line of eleven rap- and street-influenced jackets made for them by Cooper Sportswear in conjunction with the cult programme *Yo! MTV Raps!* They were sold through normal channels and backed by 30-second TV commercials on MTV. The sales projection over three years was $10–15 million.

With figures like that, TV as a sales medium can be seen as having come of age. And it is clothing – especially women's clothing – that is the TV commodity of the future. Not that fashion on TV is anything new. Elsa Klensch has hosted a fashion show on CNN for the last thirteen years. *Style with Elsa Klensch* claims over 3 million viewers, most of whom are over 50. MTV's four-year-old *House of Style*, hosted by Cindy Crawford and aimed at viewers from 12 to 34 years of age, reflects the popularity of the presenter, with an estimated viewing figure of 4.8 million. The third 'Lady of Fashion' on North American TV is Canadian Jeanne Beker, in a programme aimed at viewers in the 25–49 age group, which is beamed into 48 million households. Actress Diane Keaton has entered a partnership to form Fashion Television Associates. It would seem that everyone will soon be at it, as this new way of making money gains ground.

Is it any wonder that US *Elle* is developing a half-hour variety show, possibly to be hosted by models such as Elle Macpherson and Claudia Schiffer, to reflect 'the mixture of the magazine', according to Hachette's president David Pecker, and featuring beauty, travel, health and fashion? Could it be that, in fashion, the printed page is doomed to become secondary to the TV screen, possibly even to die? Already, TV selling has had an impact on America's $51- billion catalogue business and experts are predicting that it could kill it completely by the turn of the century. Although not entirely as a result of interactive TV shopping, it is symptomatic of how things are going that the Chicago-based Sears-Roebuck Catalog, founded over a hundred years ago, has finally bitten the dust, eliminating almost 20,000 jobs. The 'big book', as it was known, was an American institution that went into 14 million households per season. Sears executives are making no secret of the fact that they are looking at the possibilities provided by non-store retailing, especially cable TV, to take its place.

Other American institutions got there first. Following the success of individual designers such as Diane von Fürstenberg, whose TV appearances on QVC, along with a model, resulted in orders worth $1.5 million for her Silk Assets sportswear in just two hours, or Bob Mackie's four appearances that sold $850,000-worth of scarves and jewellery, those traditional monoliths of American retailing, the department stores, are moving in despite what Diller sees as a natural bias in the retail trade against TV shopping 'as there is in the early days of any medium'.

Saks Fifth Avenue was the first in signing an agreement with QVC which forged an historic link between a traditional retailer and the purveyors of new technology which could be the death warrant of department stores in the twenty-first century. The new century could dawn with QVC as the biggest fashion retailer in the world. Saks created $500,000-worth of clothes for the TV début of their Real Clothes line, introduced by Anne Keene, the store's senior vice-president, which were not obtainable through any other medium. In the first of three TV shows Saks sold $600,000-worth of merchandise.

Electronic shopping – known in the trade by the hideous name of infomercials – generated around $900 million of sales in 1993. TV Macys, owned by the famous New York store which has been fighting bankruptcy since 1992, shows clearly that traditional retailers who are in trouble are putting their faith in the new approach. As Macys' creative consultant, Don Hewitt, told *Women's Wear Daily*, 'We're going to lift this place up and put it in millions of living rooms.' The idea is not as preposterous as it sounds. Over 2.8 million American homes receive cable TV, and about half a million of those are in the New York area. How many will tune in to TV Macys in autumn 1994 when transmissions begin? Even if – as has been the pattern with TV sales so far – 40 per cent of the merchandise is returned, the venture would still be profitable for the troubled store.

It can only be a matter of time before designers join in. Already, Calvin Klein has praised his friend Diller's initiative and said, 'It would be great to be able to sell things through TV.' Can this be the next century's solution to the problems of the fashion world?

Or might it be the turn away from designer glamour exemplified by the story of The Gap? At the other end of the price range from Ralph Lauren, but selling only a slightly different version of the

Americana of jeans and sweats for which the world clamours, The Gap is the great downmarket American success story. Once described as the *Terminator 2* of retailing, the company has over 1,300 shops worldwide and, in the early 1990s, led the field for stylish, casual fashion at a sensible price – three Gap polo shirts can be bought for the price of one from Ralph Lauren. Founded in 1969 in San Francisco, The Gap originally sold rock records and surplus Levi jeans, but by 1989 had joined Brooks Bros as the only US firm to establish its store name as an important brand name. Just how important is reflected in a profit increase of almost 60 per cent in 1991 – the firm's golden year – which brought in $229,873 million. It was the reward for a deliberately different marketing ploy.

Whereas other retailers appealing to a wide age or income band concentrated on opening in shopping malls, The Gap decided that its narrow-focus, practical designs needed a different approach, and targeted downtown locations for its shops. But the very success of The Gap – and it sister company, Banana Republic – attracted fierce competition, and by the middle of 1992 things were not looking so rosy. Gap merchandise was considered lacking in variety and too reliant on basics. Esprit, Guess and Pepe were snapping at the company's heels in what has developed into an all-out jeans war as companies try to keep afloat in the recession.

New contenders in the overcrowded youth and sportswear fields spring up all the time and manage to corner a piece of the market, for a time at least, with spectacular financial results. The Los Angeles firm of BUM Equipment was founded in 1986 and grossed $2 million in its first year by concentrating on lines with a young appeal such as cotton fleece hooded sweatshirts and the ubiquitous T-shirt, promoted as 'lifestyle' dress, with advertisements using not models but real people. The approach paid off: by 1992, BUM had a turnover of $250 million.

It seems that nothing can dull the world's appetite for young, relaxed American sportswear – the sort of clothes that, as they were once aptly described, 'you can wear without having to suck in your stomach'. T-shirts and sweats – the antithesis of backward-looking French traditional dressmaking – bring ease but, more, they make people feel young and sexy. No French designer's clothes have that particular 'feel-good' factor. An outfit from Yves Saint Laurent or Claude Montana, beautifully made and perfectly designed, projects a different form of sexuality, to do with allure and seduction, neither of which has a high currency as the twenty-first century comes nearer. The world wishes to be free. Clothes must not constrain the body but, even more importantly, they must not constrain the individual. That is why American ease is at a premium.

Indigenous US brand names command almost fanatical worldwide loyalty, especially in the young. One has only to look at footwear to realise the amounts of money that can be made by American firms with a strong base in Europe. Timberland boots, the pioneers of US footwear in Europe, took $79 million of their total $226 million sales for 1991 in Europe. But it is athletic footwear from America that the world most craves. A business that ten years ago was dominated by the German firm of Adidas has fallen almost entirely to American firms, most notably Nike, which spent $63 million on European advertising in 1992, and Reebok, with a European ad budget of $50 million. Advertising pays: Nike sales in Europe are over a billion dollars a year, and are planned to reach $2.4 billion by 1996.

With traditional markets dominated by Americanisation, as well as being saturated with main and secondary lines, designers are turning not just to new retail strategies but to wholly new markets. China, in particular, has been targeted as the next exploitable retail area. Laura Biagotti has already signed a contract with a state-controlled Chinese trading company to make clothes and accessories for sale in China. For her foresight, she received the country's Marco Polo award as the first foreign designer in the

Chinese market – if one forgets Pierre Cardin, who was there in the 1970s and has shops in most major Chinese cities.

The boom economic zone is Shenzhen, close enough to Hong Kong to feel 'safe' to Westerners, but still in mainland China. It had the world's fastest-growing economy in 1992, with a gross domestic product that soared to 19 per cent. It is *the* current target for Western designers, with a boutique for Donna Karan's secondary line DKNY and the Seibu department store carrying Versace ready-to-wear, Karl Lagerfeld, Louis Vuitton, Ermenegildo Zegna and La Perla underwear. Even designers who as yet have no footing there realise the importance of the Chinese connection: in 1993 Giorgio Armani sponsored an exhibition of Chinese painters at the Venice Biennale, and Valentino and Gianfranco Ferre were guests of honour at an extravaganza in Beijing called Chic 93. Treated like visiting heads of state, they were personally greeted on arrival by the Chinese president and party secretary, Jiang Zenin. Such a distinction tells us how serious the Chinese are about making money from Western designers and how much they want to make the world forget the events in Tiananmen Square. High fashion clothes are non-political for the majority of the world, despite what minor British designers may think, and it is significant that China has chosen them as its primrose path back to Western approval.

There are clear advantages for both sides. Quite apart from the consumer potential of China's vast population, already obsessed with prestigious brand names, manufacturers need to find reliable new sources of manufacture. High wages and production costs in Western countries have made them look increasingly at non-traditional fashion manufacturing areas such as the Caribbean, Eastern Europe and even countries like Spain and Austria. In a sense, for some designers, moving to China is rather like going home. Ninety per cent of DKNY merchandise is already produced in Hong Kong, Taiwan and South Korea. The wheel has begun to turn full circle. For years the Pacific Rim was exploited as a cheap source of labour. Now the exploitation is of a different kind. The Pacific countries are seen as the saviour for a second time. Just as cheap labour made it possible for designers and manufacturers to continue selling in the West, people in the Far East are increasingly able to buy the products they make and thus take up the slack that has become a permanent aspect of trading in the West. It is an ironic situation, but nobody is stopping to reflect on that as designers scramble to get into the new markets ahead of the competition while the pickings are still rich.

Perhaps the most surprising, though also the oldest, reaction to the problems of selling enough clothes to keep a business healthy is to concentrate on selling something else altogether. At the heart of the designer scam lies the belief that fashion companies exist primarily to sell clothes. This is no longer always true, and in some cases has not been true for some time. The clothes have become secondary to other money makers, of which the prime example is perfume. Rather than trying to market the clothes, selling them becomes unimportant as long as they serve their purpose of promoting the scent. Getting someone to buy into the designer myth through a small but very expensive bottle of perfume is an altogether easier proposition than getting them to part with even more money for a suit of clothes.

It would seem, after several experiments with names of film stars and socialites such as Sophia Loren and Gloria Vanderbilt, it is the fashion designer's name that is trusted. The only exceptions are renowned firms such as Estée Lauder and stars like Elizabeth Taylor, whose names have a unique appeal to women.

But it is, of course, a con. The people who matter in perfume creation are chemists, the technicians in white coats who actually mix the ingredients and come up with the scent. But who would buy a perfume which used as its credentials a pristine, sterile laboratory and a group of scientists playing with test tubes?

Scent is the thing that virtually all women can afford in their attempts to buy into the designer dream, which is why it is so instructive as a model for the fashion and luxury goods market in its entirety. The designer scam works only with our connivance; it relies on restlessness and unease. We all remember how Grandma always smelt the same, moving in a haze of roses or lily of the valley. No such consistency is found in modern women. They have wardrobes of scent from which to choose, according to mood, time of day or expectation. We are so anxious for the glamour and kudos of the right designers' names that we respond to the latest launch advertising, the newest bottle shape, almost as reliably as if the heads of the fragrance industry were manipulating us on the end of a string. And in a way, of course, they are. They do so with our full cooperation and little consideration of value for money.

According to a survey in *W Fashion Europe*, only 11 per cent of the retail price of a bottle of scent is devoted to the ingredients and packaging. The rest is swallowed up in ways that the average buyer never considers: 32 per cent of the price goes to the retailer; 12 per cent is the manufacturer's share; 17 per cent is used for advertising and promotion; overheads take 13 per cent and the rest is for VAT – 15 per cent on average in Europe.

Carmel Snow, the great editor of *Harper's Bazaar*, once remarked that 'Nobody used dressmaker perfume until Chanel came out with her famous No. 5.' What she meant was that the great scents came direct from the world's most prestigious 'noses' without being fiddled with in order to express the whim of a fashion designer. Snow also felt that those in the know, the cognoscenti of fashion excellence, considered dressmaker perfume still slightly *déclassé*.

In the first three decades of the century, a lady would usually obtain her perfume from one of France's great parfumiers such as Coty, Houbigant, Guerlain or Caron, and it would be floral: Rose Jacqueminot, perhaps, created by Coty in 1900, or the same firm's

Muguet des Bois of 1936. Again, she might turn to Houbigant's Quelques Fleurs of 1912 or, even more likely, L'Heure Bleue, Guerlain's smash hit of the same year. Fleurs de Rocaille (Caron, 1935), Snob (Le Galion, 1937) or Elizabeth Arden's Blue Grass of 1935 were all considered suitable. Even when No. 5 *was* created in 1921 for women more interested in fashion than breeding, there was still plenty of competition from the traditional perfumiers. Jicky, the first scent to use synthetic ingredients, had been conceived by Guerlain as long ago as 1889; Houbigant's Fougère Royale had appeared seven years earlier; Chypre by Coty in 1917 and, one of the most successful of all, Mitsouko by Guerlain in 1919.

Although Chanel was one of the first designers in the field of perfume, she was not *the* first. Poiret's Rosine had been available since 1911. And Chanel soon had her competitors as dressmaker scents spilled on to the market in a continuous stream during the 1920s and 1930s: Lanvin's Arpège in 1927, Worth's Je Reviens in 1932, Patou's Moment Suprême in 1933, followed in 1935 by Joy. Scents were seen by dressmakers as useful little sidelines: clever little earners. None of them could have dreamed of how completely they would come to dominate and almost annihilate the traditional perfume scene. Similarly, despite the fact that couturiers like Worth, Lanvin and Ricci made considerable sums from their perfumes, no one in the 1920s or 1930s could have imagined how reliant on revenue from the fragrance market high fashion houses would eventually become.

Since the 1950s the triangle has slowly inverted and the couture base which was the sole *raison d'être* of Paris fashion has become the top of the triangle, supported by a solid base of perfumery and beauty products bearing the couturier's name – a base so vital to most fashion empires that its removal would cause the rest of the pyramid to collapse. The fortunes of couture and perfume are inextricably entwined.

The manufacture and sale of perfume are much less vulnerable to economic change than fashion is, but they are affected much more by the political vagaries of the world. A sudden coup or period of political unrest in a remote corner of the globe may only rate two columns in Western newspapers and a brief mention on newscasts, but it can throw the perfume industry into turmoil with hastily convened board meetings and fax machines working nonstop if that remote corner happens to be the sole – or even major – source of a vital ingredient. It is received wisdom that the Gulf War had a disastrous effect on the sale of couture dresses. Customers either failed to travel to Paris or, in the case of Middle Eastern princesses who were such good purchasers previously, felt that an interest in clothes was inappropriate for the times. But the lack of travellers also exposed a weakness in the perfume sales pyramid. Major profits are made at duty-free counters in the airports of the world. To get a perfume accepted for duty-free sale is a coup analogous to getting a novel on the Booker short list. Those that don't make the duty-free counters are considerd unlikely to make it in terms of real sales. But things changed with the Gulf War. Suddenly there was no money going into the bank: sales virtually disappeared, even at airports far removed from the theatre of war.

Even more basic was the crisis over galbanum plant sap, obtainable only from Iran and a staple ingredient of the perfume-maker's orgue. This chest normally contains about 600 natural ingredients, in addition to over 1,000 aroma chemicals, and their countries of origin show how international – and vulnerable – scent-making is. Quite apart from conflicts, natural disasters can take their toll of raw materials, just as governments do with the taxes they decide to impose. Nature is not always reliable. Tonka beans from Venezuela, ylang-ylang petals from the Comoros Islands, oakmoss from Yugoslavia (a source now totally destroyed) and tuberose are mixed with the leaves of cistus labdanum, a tree

107

native to Spain, where early supplies were obtained by combing them from the fleece of sheep. There is osmanthus from China, where petals cost 1,500 francs per kilo; and the most expensive of all ingredients, root of Tuscan iris, which takes three years in growing and needs three years of drying before it can be processed and finally put on the market at FF 500,000 per kilo.

Then there are the staples: roses and jasmine. They cost fragrance companies like Givandon-Roure and its rival, International Flavours and Fragrances, considerable sums for the top-class perfumes. Grasse roses from the French firm Charabot & Cie are considered the best. The firm has been supplying them since 1817 and they are still harvested in the same way, by hand, between 5 and 10 each morning before the dew has dried and, for the best quality, in the same month: *roses de mai* cost FF 45,000 per kilo, which is five times the price of Bulgarian roses and ten times that of Moroccan or Turkish petals. An ounce of Joy reputedly contains the petals of 28 Grasse roses and 10,600 jasmine flowers. If the jasmine comes from Grasse, it costs FF 150,000 per kilo. Egyptian jasmine is a fraction of the price now that its staple market, Russian government-owned perfumeries, has slumped since the collapse of the totalitarian state.

Expense, vulnerability, and even social pressure all dog the perfume business: whereas the secretions from civet cats and beavers, which are essential scent ingredients, can be milked humanely without damage to the animal, another important ingredient, musk from the abdominal sac of the Himalayan musk deer, can be obtained only by slaughter. Such a method is unacceptable to many markets, including the all-powerful North American one. Ambergris, the undigested fish parts ejected by whales, is as suspect as anything to do with whales is. It is interesting that the Japanese, the nation most committed to whale hunting, have little tradition of perfume wearing and consume only a small fraction of the world's supply of top fragrances.

If the fight to make a perfume seems hard it is as nothing to what is involved in ensuring that it will make an impact when it is finally produced. Many considerations must be taken into account, not least the name. Most of the best ones have already gone or been earmarked for future use. There are 91,571 fragrances registered in France alone. The top beauty company L'Oréal, whose sales reached $6.26 billion in 1991, have 50,000 trademarks registered worldwide, of which 20,000 have not yet been used. The competition for names is intense and, as most of the obvious, recognisable ones in all their permutations have long gone, companies increasingly make up names that they hope will be exotic enough to catch the imagination. Parfums Givenchy have been especially successful, although their top-selling men's fragrance, Xeryus, ran into trouble with Parfums Yves Saint Laurent, who complained that the name – originally spelled Keryus – was too close to that of Kouros, its own men's fragrance. After weeks of negotiation, Parfums Givenchy gave way and changed the K to X, but it was a close-run thing. The first shipments of Xeryus went out with labels bearing the new name stuck over the old; there was no time to reprint before launch day.

Perfume myth has it that Chanel No. 5 became a bestseller during and after World War II because it was a name that GIs in Europe could pronounce without embarrassment. The same is said of Dior perfumes in the 1950s. Beauty firms have always been conscious of pronunciation difficulties and the pitfalls inherent in having a French name spoken, for example, by an Arab. The exotic-sounding can become the obscene if they are not wary. As more of the world's population come into the commercial grasp of purveyors of luxury goods, the difficulties increase. 'How will it sound in Korean?' was not a question of great concern ten years ago, but it is now of vital interest in the boardrooms of the beauty groups. As Yves Saint Laurent's Pierre Bergé – no slouch at knocking the opposition – said when told that Calvin Klein's perfumes were poised for an assault on France, the most chauvinist of fragrance markets where 71 per cent of men's and women's fragrance sales are generated by fifteen all-French brands, 'Before they can get people to buy the fragrances, they are going to have to explain who he his and how to pronounce his name.'

That is why Parfums Yves Saint Laurent have chosen names such as Paris and Opium that are internationally safe. If a name already exists – there are international registers – it can be bought. Chanel bought Egoiste from the magazine of that name for a price reckoned to be not less than $550,000. Parfums Yves Saint Laurent bought the name Opium from two elderly perfumiers in 1977 for $200 but to secure Champagne they paid 3 million francs – and even then had to go to court in order to obtain it. At the time of writing, the battle continues, with YSL's Pierre Bergé insisting on his right to the use of the name and Bernard Arnault, whose Financière Agache conglomerate owns both Veuve Clicquot and Moët et Chandon champagne, insisting equally firmly that he has no right at all to reserve the name for a specific product.

But even when a fortune has been paid to secure a name that is no protection against plagiarism. The scent industry has much in it that stinks. In addition to animal cruelty, there are problems of piracy and fakes. Copies of the great scents are made illegally in many parts of the world. Controlling contraband manufacture of any luxury item outside Europe is difficult, and scent is no exception. Factories from Turkey to Tunis and Taiwan pump it out by the gallon to be sold on Oxford Street and its equivalents throughout Europe. In Latin America they churn it out for street vendors on Fifth Avenue and all the major cities of North America. Even within Europe, fake scent factories abound, especially in Spain and southern Italy. Local judges are happy to help neighbourhood wide boys by turning a blind eye to violations of even the most blatant kind, especially, as is usually the case, when there is handsome remuneration for doing so.

With such huge potential profits at stake, both illegal and legal, a name must be kept under wraps for as long as possible, so that it cannot be stolen. Even so, industrial espionage is widespread and a company must be very quick and very thorough to see that it has registered its new name worldwide. Once the name of a new scent is known, there is an immediate scramble by crooks eager to make a killing. They rush to register it in the remoter – and usually less well regulated – markets of the world where a little bribery here, a favour there, can work wonders in making the illegal appear kosher. They then sit back until the scent-maker approaches them to sell their right to a name that in reality should not be theirs.

Eventually the name is agreed, the sales point decided, and the scent is finally up and running. Now comes the hard part. Scents are created to be, if not everlasting, then certainly sempiternal. Unlike clothes, they should be above and beyond the local variations of fashion and the vagaries of the seasons, although the German firm Escada swam against the tide in 1993 by producing a 'summer scent', Chiffon Sorbet, in an edition of 120,000 bottles only, promising future limited editions linked to themes in the Escada collection on an annual basis.

Expensively and extravagantly launched, new perfumes must be able to last. Yet they are up against stiff competition from other companies' products, all chasing a finite share of the market, with each company being careful not to dent the sales of its own bestsellers. One has only to recall the many new fragrances launched in the Eighties and ask how many are still in existence to realise that this is a field with a failure rate higher than any other outside pop music. The US president of Parfums Givenchy commented: 'The scrolls of launches read like a list of war dead.' In autumn 1993, no fewer than 40 new fragrances for men and women were launched in North America alone. In 1983 the number was 24, in 1973 it was 13.

This prodigality leads to huge problems for new scents. In such a competitive field there is a fight for shelf room. Every duty-free store, every perfume hall, every chemist, drugstore and discount outlet wants to stock proven bestsellers and yet, at the same time, cannot risk missing out on the excitement of a launch and the subsequent sales boom generated by the promotion of a new scent. Should they let it elbow out the standard favourites, what will happen if, after the initial excitement, it settles down into a sales point less successful than the ones removed from – or at least reduced on – the shelves? Those scents that do survive will immediately become vulnerable not only to copyists, but to the discounters who are known as the 'grey' marketeers. In 1991 the European Community ruled that restrictive practices in retail pricing of perfumes was in violation of EC antitrust rules. This was a body blow in the perfumer's fight against cheap sales' points, most commonly found in Britain, where chains such as Superdrug can cut perfume prices by up to 30 per cent. In fact, with 1,500 outlets for discount fragrances (leaping to 5,000 near Christmas) the UK is top of the European grey market league (with Switzerland second). It is a market estimated to be worth at least £18 million per year compared with full-price sales of around £90 million. Following the EC lead, the British Monopolies and Mergers Commission is investigating whether or not the existing recommended retail price mechanism in perfumes is anti-competitive. If it finds in favour of abolishing it, then all the major household brands, including Givenchy, YSL and Dior, could be hoist on their own petard for making their perfumes so well known and desirable through advertising that everyone wants them. The business has to steer a fine line between the need for exclusivity that sells a scent and the need to keep their huge profit margins high.

Scent advertising is the most strongly aspirational of all. It encompasses social mores and lifestyle but, since Calvin Klein's campaigns, it is above all about attitudes to morals and sexuality.

Setting the tone is vital if a big enough audience is to be captured. How much money is spent and how it is used depends upon the audience. For example, Dune by Christian Dior could have sold to the public on the concept of deserts and their remote wildness, but a press trip to Biarritz for its pre-launch publicity set the true mood that LVMH wished to instil into the public consciousness in order to reach that magic $100 million wholesale worldwide that is the benchmark for a blockbuster. This was a sophisticated, urban scent to be worn for lunch, through dinner and on to the casino by the sort of woman who could cope with all three.

A scent enters public consciousness very quickly, and the way it does so will decide future sales. It is a 'one bite at the cherry' scenario. If it fails to find its market, if it does not come over as a unique new personality in the perfume field, it has no second chance. Publicity is vital in projecting an image that reflects the fragrance, its bottle and the packaging. But even more important and elusive is the need to project the personality of the designer whose name it carries. This is the intangible that everything else must represent if the scent is to capture the imagination. There are various ways of achieving this. Beauté Prestige International (BPI), the French perfume subsidiary of Shiseido, housed in a $15 million plant built in 1992 in the Loire to supply Europe, has placed great emphasis on bottle and packaging. L'Eau d'Issey, the perfume of cult Japanese designer Issey Miyake, whose name is revered in fashion circles but barely causes a ripple beyond, was given a bottle, created by Alain de Mourgues, meant to invoke the rather esoteric appeal of a Miyake dress. The name, a pun on 'Odyssey', focused on the designer's Christian name because in many cultures Miyake presented a pronunciation difficulty. But even with a publicity campaign photographed by Irving Penn, it is a scent with only limited appeal, so lacking in common resonance is Miyake's name.

For Jean Paul Gaultier's perfume, BPI took a completely different approach, guided by the designer, who was determined from the outset to create a perfume that reflected his approach to women and their sexuality. In contrast to L'Eau d'Issey's elegant, understated white card origami pyramid, Gaultier's scent was presented in a tin can modelled on a baked beans tin and stamped with Gaultier's name as dockside containers are. The message was no-frills, no-fuss utilitarianism. But inside, all was saucy voluptuousness, with the pink perfume in a bottle in the shape of a woman's torso wearing a corset. The spray was released by pulling a tab exactly like those found on beer and soft-drink cans. The whole concept brilliantly realised the preoccupations, peccadilloes and predilections of Gaultier by highlighting the perversity and desire to shock that the public perceives as his persona. The scent was an immediate hit with young women throughout Europe, becoming a best-seller in Germany, France and the United Kingdom.

Few designers dare be so bold. Flights of fancy are tightly controlled. For Wings, the scent launched by Giorgio of Beverly Hills in 1992, a slender female statuette which came to be known as Ashley was created to help set the mood of the fragrance. Used in window displays, it was guaranteed to upset nobody, it was so unremarkable. Other companies are more imaginative – or more desperate. To give Oscar de la Renta's Volupté a send-off in Germany, Sanofi Beauté produced giant scented posters to wrap around 1,000 advertising columns in Germany's eighteen major cities. Pierre Cardin launched Rose Cardin in 1992 at Galeries Lafayette in Trump Tower by having customers greeted by girls dressed in Cardin couture and carrying platters piled high with silk roses doused in the perfume to take home as souvenirs.

Although, paradoxically, the actual smell of a perfume is less important for sales than it was fifty years ago – the packaging, publicity and aura of the designer being equally important selling points – it is clearly essential to get people to sniff it and, increasingly, this is done long before a potential customer walks up to a counter. The most effective way of achieving this is by inserting scented strips into high-quality magazines. Virtually every women's magazine has carried them and even *Vanity Fair*, which banished them in a blaze of publicity a few years ago, has taken them back into the fold. For Ralph Lauren's Safari, 48 million strips were inserted in magazines over a ten-month period in 1990. For Safari for Men in 1992, Cosmair – owners of Lauren perfume – inserted 35 million over five months as part of a promotion and advertising budget estimated at $18 million. To break into the French market, known as The Cemetery for American fragrances, Calvin Klein's Eternity was given an initial budget of $5 million in 1993 which paid for 25 million scented strips, 15,000 posters (1,500 for Paris alone) and a series of 10-page advertisements in *Elle*, *Marie-Claire* and *Vogue*, backed up by a TV campaign featuring supermodel Christy Turlington playing with children on a beach.

Scented strips are a proven and effective way of gaining publicity. But there are other, cheaper ways. One of the best things with which to start a movement that leads to a campaign is to do something that will excite fashion insiders and make them talk. This talk is quickly caught up by the media, who carry on the process of taking the name to a wider audience. In 1993 Paco Rabanne decided on this path in order to get people talking about his XS Excess Pour Homme. In what he called a form of subliminal advertising, he sent out to parties models with XS in temporary tattoos across their bosoms. He ensured that his models were always to the front at the right *vernissage*, always sitting next to the man most likely to be photographed at a fashionable dinner, and always left the most swinging disco on the correct arm. The paparazzi loved it and the XS girls kept everybody guessing. Rabanne followed this up with a $4 million TV campaign and a video by PolyGram for a pop song called 'Perfume Paranoia' on Channel M 6's music video show.

For Safari for Men, Ralph Lauren went one stage further, appearing in his own TV advertising campaign, which swallowed a third of the $17 million earmarked for the launch. Dressed in his signature cowboy denim and a stetson, Lauren was seen riding through a meadow on Long Island and then galloping along the beach, his horse's hooves splashing through the water in the traditional fashion. The whole mood, meant to symbolise the perfume's slogan, 'Living without boundaries', was geared to reinforcing Lauren's attitudes and philosophies. The concept of the TV films came from the designer himself. For Armani's Giò, L'Oréal took a different tack, commissioning *Twin Peaks'* director David Lynch to create the TV advertisement starring actress-model Lara Harris and asking the question, 'Who is Giò?'

The North American launch of Giò in 1993 was a carefully orchestrated affair recognising the fact that the home-grown competition was already considerable and expecting a certain amount of consumer resistance to a name that conveyed little and was not easily pronounced. It also had to overcome the differences in scent tastes between Europe and the US. Although perfume is becoming global, with homogenised fragrances that will appeal to the widest possible market, regional preferences still linger. European-style scents are very balanced, with no predominant notes, whereas American taste favours flat top notes and wide bottom notes. Taking this and other possible difficulties into account, Giò was very carefully priced for the American market, at a price below Opium, Paris and Chanel No. 5, but slightly above other new scents such as Dior's Dune and Givenchy's Amarige. It was hoped that Giò would move from the niche band where most European brands stick in America to the position of a major fragrance power. To help things along, its launch fitted in with the A/X Armani Exchange début and the magazine ad campaign was photographed by Peter Lindbergh. Final icing on the publicity cake was a New York showing of Armani's collection – the first in eleven years. The promotional budget for the Giò launch was $50 million, and the projected annual total at wholesale was $100 million.

With such sums involved it is not surprising that nearly all major designer scents are owned by big beauty conglomerates. They are the only people with the money not only to launch a scent but also to set up the infrastructure, supply lines and support required in order to keep it ahead in the race for sales.

They straddle the world, all powerful. Yet their names, even if known to the public, are never associated with the glamour products that bring them such kudos and cash. These international conglomerates own the top names in fashion and perfumery; they are the angels and fairy godmothers whose cash bails designers out of tricky situations but whose power when things go wrong is wielded with the ruthless indifference of a Samurai's sword.

Mention Unilever or Procter and Gamble to most people and they will immediately think of washing powder or downmarket brands of toilet soap. And yet, between them, these two firms own and control some of the most exclusive and glamorous names in perfumery. Unilever, based in London and Rotterdam, owns Elizabeth Arden and has a blue chip portfolio of top perfumes including all Calvin Klein's brands, Parfums Lagerfeld, Cerruti, Valentino, and the international best seller, White Diamonds by Elizabeth Taylor. In 1992, Unilever beauty sales reached $5.086 billion. Procter and Gamble of Cincinnati, Ohio, owns Max Factor, Old Spice, Hugo Boss parfum, Laura Biagotti perfumes and a host of beauty and hair products including Oil of Ulay and Head and Shoulders, which together generated estimated sales in the region of $5 billion in 1992.

But it is L'Oréal, with beauty sales of $7.456 billion, that is ranked number one. Based in France, at Clichy, it owns Lancôme, Helena Rubenstein, Laboratoires Garnier and the perfume ranges of Ralph Lauren, Giorgio Armani, Paloma Picasso and Guy

Laroche. In 1991 L'Oréal added new locations to its conquest of the world when it opened shops in Prague and Kiev, following this up in 1992 with the launch of its first Russian designer fragrance, Maroussia by Slava Zaitsev, produced in Moscow to fill a gap created by the collapse of state-owned perfume companies since the breakdown of communism. It is firms like L'Oréal, Procter and Gamble and Unilever who lead the field in promotion, devoting ever bigger budgets to the launch of new lines, laying out terrifyingly large sums to get back even more, and usually succeeding. They are companies which make bank managers smile, but they are not unique. The world of international fragrances is a large one and includes many well-known names. Estée Lauder of New York, whose scent Spellbound produced disappointing figures in 1992 which have been recovered to an extent by the launch of Aramis's Tuscany Per Donna in 1993, has total beauty sales of almost $3 billion. Wella, the German group that has been in business for over a hundred years, owns Parfums Rochas and, like L'Oréal, has expanded into what was Russia with a Wella salon in Moscow.

The Chanel group, with an annual sales total for beauty and perfume products in excess of $500 million, is still privately owned by the Wertheimer family and underwrites the cost of Chanel couture from the sales of its products. In 1991 Chanel introduced Coco, with a controversial ad campaign conceived by Jean-Paul Goude featuring pop singer Vanessa Paradis as a caged songbird; and, for men, Egoiste, also filmed by Goude, whose style and panache – as you would expect from the man who 'caged' Grace Jones – delighted and shocked in about the same measure. What Chanel herself would feel about an advertisement featuring a girl swinging from a perch like Tweetie Pie, complete with feathered tail and red silk rope tied around her ankle, and a slogan, L'Esprit de Chanel, is frightening to contemplate – but it clearly pleases the Wertheimers, who know a seller when they see one.

7

The Catwalk Conspiracy

Critics view the fashion world as trivial and meretricious and cite as evidence the fashion shows that take place with the maximum of publicity and the minimum of dignity every season around the world. Even the most partisan fashion supporter knows that the critics have a point. Fashion shows are at the core of the falseness and double-dealing that are the designer scam. They demonstrate more clearly than anything else the deception which embroils the fashion industry in its attempts to keep us thinking 'designer' and buying the clothes that bear the label.

Although fashion shows are presented as exercises in glamour, they are, in reality, cynical and manipulative window-dressing of the most blatant kind. Their purpose is to hide the reality of a business which, in the 1990s, is coming apart at the seams almost as quickly as many a designer jacket of the 1980s. These shows pinpoint a deep malaise in the fashion world, which is that the commentators and critics – whose vigilance should protect us, the consumers – can be conned into accepting anything and lauding it to the skies provided it is on a runway and the music is right.

It is no accident that, alone of the minor creative arts, fashion has victims, defined by the *Oxford English Dictionary* as living creatures 'offered as a sacrifice to some deity or supernatural power'. It is an eerily appropriate definition of the majority of fashion commentators. Their relationship with designers and the fashion trade is so convoluted, multi-level and confused that it is hard to know which side is conning the other. But behind the whirl and hype of the shows is the indisputable fact that what appears on the runway frequently has little to do with the way fashion is moving. The items chosen to be photographed and written about are usually remarkable in their irrelevance to true fashion development. Like children, the fashion-victim press stretches out eagerly to the most glittering and gaudy of items, totally forgetting that most women of sound mind require something rather more substantial.

The vast majority of designers' ideas die a sterile death. In the case of the fashion shows, this is entirely intentional. Today's shows take the old aphorism that the only good dress is a bought dress and make a mockery of it; the only good dress is the photographed or reported dress. Only a handful of the clothes seen on the runway will actually go into production. The majority are merely there to generate excitement. A report from *Women's Wear Daily* of a show in November 1992 neatly encapsulates the policy: 'Many of the audience were confused . . . but retailers had been told in advance that there would be plenty of other pieces in the showroom.'

Carry a copy of the 'Collections' issue of *Vogue* when you visit the designer shops of Sloane Street or Madison Avenue and see how many of the clothes pictured will be hanging on the racks in a reasonably wide range of sizes. Probably none. It is becoming hard to find a designer shop that devotes even a quarter of its selling and display space to the main-line collections. Recession has forced designers to turn to diffusion or secondary lines which deliberately eschew design originality and novelty for bread-and-butter wearability at a more affordable price, but still with the cachet of the designer's name. The whiz-bang fun of the show has less and less connection with what is available in the shops. The cost of originality in lost sales is too great a risk to take.

It has not always been so. The nature of fashion shows was different in the couture years. They were predominantly occasions for private customers to see the new line and decide which models they would choose to have the couturier make for them. The press was given the briefest look-in, almost on sufferance, at the first presentation, in essence often a dress rehearsal for the more important shows for private customers that were to follow. From the 1930s to the 1960s, fashion shows were decorous affairs where each model was shown in silence – a silence intensified by the acute concentration of the audience – by a mannequin who rarely smiled and did not consider it part of her role to ingratiate herself or interact with those watching the show. The showbiz element was completely lacking. Dresses were displayed with monastic severity. But the shows were still very much social affairs, often taking place in the evening at the cocktail hour with an audience dressed to the hilt as if for a gala at the opera or a *vernissage*. And, of course, they did not come merely to look. They came to buy.

Times changed, and by the mid-1960s there were no longer enough rich women willing to support couture. The tiny gilt chair – symbol of the past – was replaced by a moulded plastic one hired for the occasion. The democratisation of the fashion show had begun, even if the vulgarisation was still some way off.

Ready-to-wear fashion is based on a totally different premise from that of couture. Designers must sell clothing in vast numbers in order to cover the costs of a modern dressmaking establishment – exclusivity is no longer part of the equation. Neither is secrecy. The old paranoia over piracy has been replaced by the new – fear of not getting as much coverage as one's rivals. Today, the sooner the world knows what a designer has to offer the better, so that buyers from every level of the garment industry can beat a path to his door. Publicity is the life-blood of the enterprise, and publicity only comes to the new and extreme. Clothes must be seen but, more importantly, they must be *presented* – that is, grouped to make a statement, introduced in an order which makes the designer's thinking clear and, of course, shown in a manner that excites the audience to buy or, especially important to modern designers, to write about them in such a way that those who have not seen the show are stimulated to rush out and buy when the watered down versions of the new line arrive in boutiques and stores around the world.

This has affected not only the nature of the shows, but, because of the new demands, the nature of fashion itself. Slow-moving, logical development of a fashion philosophy honed and refined over several seasons was the way of couture in the past: Chanel's suits in the Fifties were a constantly revisited series of variations on a theme; Balenciaga's slow deconstruction of the tailored suit took almost five years to achieve; even Dior's Forties' New Look was the logical continuation of the mood of the late Thirties that had been only temporarily destroyed by the privations of wartime. The customers who bought their clothes from the great couturiers did not want a bomb dropped into their wardrobe; they wished to add new items of clothing that would augment, not outdate, those they already possessed. They would have been irritated, not stimulated, by a couturier who changed direction each season, considering him immature and artistically barren. Now, novelty is all. The commercial backing necessary for ready-to-wear gives its blessing today to what would have been crimes forty years ago. Novelty is what the media needs in order to stimulate public interest. The fashion show is still the most dramatic way of catching attention.

And it is self-perpetuating. Despite the astronomical bills, the extraordinary demands on time, the diversion from the job of making clothes that are actually to sell, every designer who can afford one has one. As a form of publicity, its cost-effectiveness has often been called into question, but everybody is scared to buck the trend. Nobody has the nerve to dispense with a show, just as nobody has the wisdom to come up with a viable alternative.

In the mid-1980s, Giorgio Armani alone tried to break the pattern. For one season, he decided not to have a runway show. In its place, the press were invited to view videos and tableaux of clothes. Armani let it be known that in his opinion traditional fashion shows were too costly and inefficient as a method of disseminating ideas; they were an inconvenient break in the rhythm of the dress house year and, above all, they often bore no relation to the clothes that were actually found in the shops.

In all points, he was correct. His attitude was as logical as it was modern. Producing many variations on a theme merely to 'fill out' a show is clearly inefficient; spending a fortune on models, music and all the backstage support required is a costly waste; production schedules and working programmes could be much more efficiently organised if preparations for a show did not interrupt them; the clothes on the runway are, all too often, extravagant eye-catchers far removed from the lines that go into production for the following season.

Intellectually, Armani could not be faulted. And yet, it was a misjudgement. Far from following his logic, the fashion world was appalled. He forgot that fashion – and especially fashion reporting – has nothing to do with logic or common sense, and is essentially emotional. Next season, his clothes were back on the runway.

A fashion show has drama and glamour. Even more, it has status. Armani took all three away. He overestimated the professional standards of the media by assuming that they would have sufficient fashion intelligence to see his design story without a variety show to lead them. The press were put out, didn't understand, felt lost and betrayed without the bread and circus show. They did not want to use their brains. Like small children, they wanted something bright, bouncy and loud to watch or – as Armani's shows never delivered such things anyway – at least moving, living figures to engage their attention.

There was another spur to their resentment. Half the appeal of a show isn't what goes on on the runway, but what goes on in the audience. Journalists enjoy the drama of a fashion show for what happens to *them* in the hectic hour devoted to getting into the show space, watching the show and then getting out again. To understand why, we need first to appreciate the horrific experience that it is to be in the audience of a ready-to-wear show: an experience more hair-raising than anything at Alton Towers.

Ready-to-wear fashion shows have generally been held in vast temporary tents in Paris and London, although Paris has recently acquired a newly constructed, permanent exhibition space at the Louvre, like the Fiera in Milan, where the Italian shows take place. Until recently, New York shows were held in showrooms, lofts, theatres and all sorts of odd spaces, but in November 1993 the situation was bought under control with the inauguration of '7th on Sixth', a tented village erected in Bryant Park to centralise the shows. But, no matter where they are held, fashion shows have a common theme: they bring together far too many people in one place and them attempt to squeeze them through entrances narrow enough for security to control who gets in – and who does not. Fashion show organisers – especially in Europe – *adore* security control not, as one might imagine, in order to check for guns and bombs, but so that they can push home the message that those who follow the drumbeat of fashion are – no matter how exalted – merely the footsoldiers, cannon fodder of the industry as far as the designer is concerned.

Picture the scene. Well over a thousand people are kept waiting for at least 20 minutes – and often much longer – in a space that can comfortably take 400. They are pressed together like sheep on the way to slaughter. In London and, until recently, Paris, they are frequently crushed into outside pens with rain bucketing down on their expensive designer clothes. The journalists and buyers are watched contemptuously by the PR people and house managers on the other side of the fence in their warm, dry and spacious area behind the rows of security guards as even the most exalted of the guests are pressed tighter together by the eager latecomers at the back of the crowd. In this one respect, fashion is egalitarian. There is no pecking order in this crush, and no special privileges. Contempt is impartial. The edict is stern: all, including the grandest, must pass through this crush as a cleansing fire, a form of necessary purification, before becoming worthy to behold the works of the maestro. Mortification of the flesh, after all, is an essential preliminary for those who wish to enter Heaven. Horror stories abound about behaviour in the crush: a British fashion journalist faints in the confusion outside the tents in Paris. As she slides gently to the floor, her fellow Brits support her as best they can with their own arms pinioned to their sides. Help appears to be at hand. A Frenchman leans forward, looks down at the inert figure. Has relief come at last? The crush opens slightly for him. He bends down. The journalist's eyes flicker their gratitude. Gallic fingers deftly remove the prized invitation from her lifeless grasp and the figure disappears without offering succour. Before giving way to moral outrage remember that this is a ruthless kill-or-be-killed world, and an invitation to a top show is a prize indeed. God-given opportunities must not be spurned.

Not that possession of an invitation necessarily makes it easy to enter. Even editors of *Vogue* have been forced into fist fights with guards who cannot – or will not – recognise the importance of their entourage, just as English-speaking journalists refuse to acknowledge that many people do not speak their language and become very tetchy when they do not. In the pushing and shoving, an awkward guard who is really trying to annoy can delay things sufficiently to get tempers boiling, but the people with the real power to humiliate are the designer's PR women who, queens for a day, take full advantage of a situation which they have in many ways worked to create – a situation that briefly reverses roles and gives *them* the whip-hand.

This is what was missing from Armani's vision. This is theatre, performance art, with the audience as key participants. Like penitents carrying a cross in Easter processions or pilgrims crawling on hands and knees to a shrine, fashion journalists were appalled at a future that precluded the spiritual debasement and ritual humiliation that is a vital necessity for true fashion aficionados. Fashion journalists seem to love being humiliated. They need to be treated with contempt in order to experience the full excitement of their calling and to convince themselves that they are 'cutting it' at the very edge of the creative maelstrom. And the fashion show gives them what they require. Nowhere is this more true than at the international ready-to-wear collections where hysteria runs high, tempers flare, reputations are shredded and petulance is out of control. Everyone has a marvellous time.

The pantomime begins before the shows, with the invitations and the seating plans. Here the in-house PR woman, along with the designer's personal assistant, has her first opportunity to exercise her power. Many more people wish to attend than can be accommodated. A balance must be struck between nations, magazines, newspapers, major retail stores, boutiques and manufacturers. Long lists of names are compiled. Journalists are grouped by publication and a complicated series of *aides-mémoires* is used so that freelances can be identified: those who wrote well about the designer last season can be differentiated from those who were lukewarm; and those who are so eminent that they must be present can be pinpointed. There is a brisk trade in magic markers as lists are scrutinised by members of the organisation – including the designer – whose preferences alter the pecking order, add new names and remove old ones until the final version is reached and invitations are written.

The fashion world is based on the snobbery of who is in and what is out. Seats equal status. Far too many journalists are more concerned about their placement than the clothes they have come to see. The closer to the front one sits, the more important one is. It's that simple. With a sensitivity to status as delicate as the readings of a brain scanner, the PR woman attempts to keep the clients happy as well as fulfilling the demands of the house. Each season, she knows she will fail. Someone will be misplaced; somebody's seat will entirely disappear and at least a dozen guests will complain that they have been mistreated – insulted, even – by being given the wrong places. Seating on one side of the runway is reserved for buyers, manufacturers, friends of the house, possibly private customers and, in the front row, the great and the good – ladies who lunch, pop stars, politicians and their wives – whose presence will help to obtain press and TV coverage. But placing these people is an easy task compared with seating the press on the other side of the runway.

On the international scale, it is simple enough. Every country has its top newspapers and journals whose status produces an automatic hierarchy as far as seniority is concerned. In the case of all *Vogues* and *Harpers* there is little difficulty. Even the dimmest in-house PR person has heard of them. The same is true of any newspaper with the word 'Times' in its title. Where confusion arises is with magazines like the British *Tatler*, or the American *Town and Country*. How are they to be rated? Are they front or second row? Again, *The Times* is the one British newspaper which stands for quality in foreign fashion circles, even though it bewilders the French and Italians when the writing fails to live up to such a prestigious title. So what do they do? Turn to the *Independent*, with its constantly changing fashion editors, or the *Guardian*, with no fashion editor at all? They usually do neither, shrug their shoulders and concentrate on their indigenous press and the Americans, both of whom are much more important to them.

There are certain things that do not change, however. US *Vogue* and *Women's Wear Daily* are considered the most important publications in the world as far as fashion is concerned, so they are given pride of place in the front row – usually at the end of the runway where they can see and clearly be seen. Anna Wintour, current editor of American *Vogue*, holds the central position with John Fairchild, owner and publisher of *WWD* and *W*. Nearby will be the editor of *Harper's Bazaar* – currently Liz Tilberis – and Suzy Menkes of the *International Herald Tribune*, along with the fashion editors of the *Washington Post*, *New York Times* and the other major American newspapers. The editors of French, Italian and, if space permits, British *Vogue* and *Harpers* will also be there, alongside the editors of the French edition of *Marie Claire* and French and US editions of *Elle*. Normally the British editors of those magazines will be in the front row too. Then it becomes a free-for-all, with regional variations. In Paris, more French newspaper fashion editors will be 'front-rowed'; in Italy, more Italian.

The second row is usually taken up by the fashion editors of major newspapers. Here will be found the representatives of the British broadsheets and some of the tabloids, such as the *Daily Mail* or the *Daily Express*. Others, such as the *Evening Standard*, are likely to be further back in that murky middle ground occupied by the likes of *Options*, *Cosmopolitan* and *Woman's Journal*, several rows behind *Tatler*. The process can become a little haphazard. Ignorance of changes within magazines and newspapers; inability to sift out the journalists who actually write as opposed to those who style pictures; sheer laziness or cussedness (not unknown, even in the most grandly efficient house) often lead to temper tantrums and can mean that a journalist expected to file copy immediately after the show is herded at the back or in the gangways – which are never kept clear, despite fire regulations – along with gate-crashers, groupies, well-wishers *et al.*, balancing her notepad as best she can. This is treatment that would be accepted by no other profession.

It is not always unintentional when a particular journalist is treated badly. Even one as exalted as Suzy Menkes is snubbed if she has the temerity to be too critical. She has been banned from

Dior, Versace and quite a few other eminent showings in her time. Why? you might ask. Do they hope to bring her to heel? To manipulate her into saying what they wish to hear? The answer is that, in an ideal world, for the designer, the journalist *would* be brought to heel. But Suzy does not write for the *Nether Wallop Gazette.* The *International Herald Tribune* is too important not to be present at a show. Better to be panned in such a newspaper than not to appear in its columns at all. The couturier soon relents. Kissing and making up are part of the fun.

No, the slap to Suzy is meant for other, lesser mortals – the ones who sit nervously in the second or third row fearing that they may be moved further back at any moment so that their seat may be given to someone from a more august publication. Fashion editors of downmarket tabloids or the more arcane broadsheets are vulnerable, as are the fashion editors of all but the top magazines from any country. They are the ones who learn early that, although being nice to the maestro can pay dividends in personal kudos and esteem (as well as gifts) the person to whom they really have to toady is the PR.

The front-row, first-division girls know no such fears – although, if they are honest, they will recall the days when they did. There can be few fashion journalists who have not watched, heart in mouth, as a fierce PR assistant bears down, about to expose the fact that she has stolen the seat clearly allocated to somebody else, or guiltily longed for the kindly dimming of the lights and the beginning of the show that will distract the attention of the 'seaters' from the fact that she is palpably not Herr Flugel of Cologne, whose name card lies crumpled at the bottom of her bag. But, as a journalist becomes more eminent, she has her own allotted place. Anna Wintour of US *Vogue* and Liz Tilberis of *Harper's Bazaar* are treated like goddesses.

Also somewhere near the front, if not making the front row, will be the publishers and advertising managers of the top 'glamour' magazines who are present solely to stimulate advertising revenue and to massage the ego of the designer. They usually fall asleep after the fourth or fifth show of the day, especially if they have had a heavy lunch and the clothes are not particularly sexy. They are the hollow men of fashion, yet they are treated with great deference by PRs who think they have a say in what is featured in the magazine.

Fashion editors in the front row cannot fall asleep, even if they wished to. In the old days of Fifties' grandeur, Carmel Snow was frequently known to drift off on her front- row couch, but legend had it that a sixth sense made her eyes snap open whenever something important came out. The reason why modern front-rowers find it hard to sleep has less to do with the quality of the clothes or the pace of the show than with the earth-shaking volume of the sound system, the baking heat of the lights, and, of course, the kaleidoscope of pattern swirling round on the runway above them. Anna Wintour of *Vogue* wears sunglasses – a perverse insult to a designer who has worked hard to balance and contrast his colours – and there is some speculation about whether or not her eyes may occasionally close. But editorial eyes are usually innocent eyes – always hopeful that something exciting will appear.

In this world, extravagance – of reaction, behaviour and language – is the name of the game. The Americans do it best. Chief hysteria hyper is the American journalist Polly Mellen, one-time senior fashion editor of US *Vogue*. She was trained by Diana Vreeland – of whom it was claimed that 'She can smell out a coming fashion so far ahead that she makes a bloodhound look like something with asthma' – and has copied many of the outrageous attitudes of her mentor. But where Vreeland had dignity, Mellen has impudence. She leaps up to feel materials as models stride past; stands up and claps outfits that excite her; she plays entirely by her own rules. Such behaviour passes in the world of fashion as character. American fashion illustrator Jo Eula lets his opinions be known as clearly, often by using non-regulation language when he finds a collection disappointing. Italian journalists frequently cry. The French and English sit decorously, with prim lips, whilst the Germans applaud rather too loudly at all the wrong times.

Some of the extravagance may result from the general stress of collection time. Crisscrossing a foreign city, ordering taxis in a language not entirely understood, or endlessly arguing with officials, wears down all but the toughest. The beating and battering – mental and physical – eventually take their toll. Nicholas Coleridge, managing director of Condé Nast Publications Ltd, whose stable includes *Vogue* and *Tatler*, has written that all fashion editors are more or less mad. Considering all they are put through, is it surprising that they gradually begin to crack?

Although madness strikes most dramatically at collection time, it is fuelled all year round by the fear that haunts all fashion journalists. They are conscious that they are largely irrelevant, except to the designers – who frequently look on them as nothing more than an extension of their public relations system. What haunts fashion journalists in the wee small hours is the fear that nobody is reading them.

Collection Derangement Syndrome hits most journalists at one time or another. Consider the journalist whose Milan hotel room was broken into. All her clothes were stolen. Naturally, she was shocked. What woman wouldn't be when robbed of a costly designer wardrobe with expensive jewellery and accessories to match? Later that day she took me to one side and informed me that she knew who the culprit was. Looking around guiltily in case we were being overheard, I urged her to tell. 'Well,' she said, dropping her head conspiratorially, 'I don't know whether you have noticed, but I have very large feet for a woman.' Clearly I was meant to draw a conclusion. I began to blush. My palms sweated. Did she think it was me? Finally, she spoke. 'I must have been followed to the hotel by a transvestite,' she said, adding, 'They have great difficulty in finding fashionable shoes, you know. He must have heard me ask for my key, memorised the number and then asked for it when I was out.'

When under stress, our basic characteristics surface as a protective security blanket against the strain. I recall the fashion editor of a minor English magazine, who in all the *Sturm und Drang* of collection fever made her own little nest, safe and familiar, by taking out her knitting as she waited for the shows to begin. No matter how elegant the surroundings, how impossibly sophisticated the audience, by a click of her needles she could reduce the grandest couturier's salon to the level of a suburban doctor's waiting room. It was her way to survive Collection Derangement Syndrome.

Stress also has its more sinister side. By far the most powerful force in fashion journalism is greed. I have witnessed women stealing the cheap T-shirt or minute bottle of cologne placed on chairs as a little gift for journalists, not just in ones or twos, but scooping them up from almost a complete row as if their lives depended on it. What do they do with the spoils? I know of at least one British journalist, who accepts all the samples of new products provided for her to test, use and examine before giving her professional judgement, who promptly sells them to a market stall holder. Perhaps the well-paid goody-gobblers at the collections do the same. . . .

After a show, it is customary for important journalists and fashion people to go behind the scenes to congratulate the designer. These are occasions of great emotion and almost over-whelming hypocrisy. On one occasion the designer for whom I was working responded to an eminent Italian journalist's com-ment that the shoes worn in the show were 'divine' by saying, 'Have a pair, darling.' The woman ran to where the shoes had been thrown in a confused pile. I watched, fascinated, as she shovelled the shoes, regardless of matching style, colour or size, into two enormous bags.

Fashion shows attract hangers-on in awesome numbers. They are the ones who clog up the entrance; attempt to gate-crash; forge or steal invitations and generally make life a nightmare for the organisers. Skilled at guerrilla warfare, their determination is equalled only by their cunning. They come in all languages and sexes. The most innocuous-looking but ultimately most ruthless are the groups of willowy young men, dressed in a pantomime pastiche of the looks promulgated by the latest avant-garde designer, talking excitedly about fashion personalities and laughing gaily in attention-drawing falsettos. So harmless and amusing – until they storm the barricades, and their tostesterone count shoots up.

An equally powerful group found in Paris, Milan and London are students from British art colleges. They are sent over by their lecturers and told to get into as many shows as they can. Primary offenders are the academic staff of Central, St Martin's and Kingston Polytechnic, but they are not alone. Luckily, it is a problem almost exclusively confined to British educational establishments. Other countries have more understanding of and respect for what a fashion show is: an occasion for work which, beneath all the hysteria, is aimed at professionals, not students.

That is why the industry persists with the twice-yearly shows, despite the costs. *W. Fashion Europe* estimated in 1991 that the total bill for the shows in Paris and Milan touched $50 million per season, a figure which included samples at around $12 million; and travel and lodging for staff, models and photographers at another $12 million (most models insist on club-class flights and four-star hotels as a minimum). Photographers' fees, film and processing about 250,000 rolls come at about $10 million; while show services such as music, flowers, electricians and dressers account for a further $6 million. Individual designers expect a bill of around $160,000 a show, of which rental of a space (around $40,000) and payment for models (around $60,000) are the major outlay. It also includes vital but often forgotten expenses: ushering ($2,200), pressing ($350) and invitations ($5,000). Add the cost of press dossiers (almost $17,000), gifts on seats ($1,790) and music ($3,400), for front-of-house expenses and dressers ($2,500) and hairdressers ($8,500) behind the scenes, and it becomes clear that a show is a major investment. But the industry still sees it as the most efficient way of getting across each season's message to the 700 foreign buyers, 1,800 journalists and 700 photographers who converge on Paris and Milan.

Things are different in the rarefied world of couture, which attracts considerably fewer journalists. Buyers from stores and mass-manufacturing companies attend in very much smaller numbers. This results in altogether more manageable guest lists. Most shows take place in the relative comfort of ballrooms in the de-luxe hotels that cluster around the Place Vendôme and the rue de Rivoli. The Chanel couture show, considered by many to be the most important in Paris and the one for which journalists eagerly wait, takes place in the Ecole des Beaux Arts, a suitably unusual setting for the work of such an unexpected couturier as Lagerfeld, before an audience less than quarter the size for a Chanel ready-to-wear show. The world's senior press are, of course, present, but this is a comparatively civilised way of showing clothes so, alongside professionals like Suzy Menkes, any designer worth his salt can pull in a few film stars and socialites to add éclat to the occasion. They are placed in the front row as a flesh and blood insurance policy. Even if the clothes do not find favour with photographers, the stars will, and press coverage is guaranteed. But above all it is at couture shows that the glam Yankees – eye-wateringly rich New York matrons of fashion – come into their own.

Facelifted smiles are tirelessly switched on for photographers; pipe-cleaner legs, stripped of all veins even vaguely varicose, sashay from one grand hotel to another as the shows unfold; enthusiasm gleams from every eye. These are the professional clothes consumers, the women who actually order outfits costing up to and, in some cases, over, $20,000. Their presence adds a tinsel shine to the show that no couturier lightly eschews. Their favourites are Ungaro, Valentino, Yves Saint Laurent and, latterly, Oscar de la Renta at Balmain, all of whom understand the needs of middle-aged women trapped in the amber of eternal youth.

Ivana Trump and the ladies who lunch gladly play musical chairs at their favourite shows. They have been known to whip back to their hotels and change outfits more than twice a day in order to honour their favourite couturiers by appearing in their creations at their shows. Their trim bottoms rise slightly from their chairs as the models appear, and they decide just how many dollars they will spend on creations that will probably be worn less than a dozen times. No wonder they rate such affectionate kisses from the couturiers.

The press are greeted less fulsomely, even though it was they who gave the new couture its credentials in the Eighties by parroting – and apparently believing – the assertions of one or two designers that couture was important as a laboratory for new ideas, which could flow free of the commercial constraints of ready-to-wear. It was a nice piece of manipulative argument and an excellent justification for a spectacle more linked to perfume and make-up sales than clothes, but it was sophistry as far as it related to the styles, shapes and lengths worn by women on all but the world's most fashionable streets. What can be worn slipping out of a limousine in Sloane Street does not work quite so well at a wet and windy bus stop in Gateshead. No, the real influence of the couture shows is in colour and fabric. That's where innovations are tried out. The rag trade, which supports many different forecasting agencies working two or more seasons ahead, picks up on couture patterns, prints and weaves and adapts them for the cheaper end of the market. It is not only clothes: jewellery bought at sensible prices at Christmas is almost always adapted from designs first shown at couture two winters ago, and probably not put into production then. This, if anything, is the true purpose of couture for the trade: it tells everyone what is coming next in colours, fabrics and accessories.

The best of all the couture shows is that of Yves Saint Laurent, always held in the Intercontinental Hotel. Beneath the chandeliers stretches a seemingly endless runway, its entrance framed by a baroque flower arrangement stretching up to the ceiling. At the side is the velvet curtain through which Saint Laurent's eye can be seen squinting, as he waits for people to be seated and notes who has arrived. Eventually all is ready. Pierre Bergé makes a final check, the show begins and out the models come, walking with a special slow Saint Laurent walk, half gentle charm, half dignity.

To witness a Saint Laurent show is to undergo a rich experience that carries one back to the days when couture *was* the wellspring of all fashion development, and the only criterion was to ensure that everything was perfect. Saint Laurent is the true artist of Paris fashion down whose runway in the last thirty years have come some of the most beautiful and memorable creations in the history of couture. No wonder so many of the audience are in tears by the end of the show. As a French journalist once said to me, 'What will fashion be when Yves has gone?' Judging by what currently passes as couture, the answer will be: a pathetic and vulgar thing.

The elegance and refinement of a Saint Laurent couture show are a far cry from the scrum of ready-to-wear. But even there, the chaos in the tent finally subsides and something like order prevails. Everyone is more or less seated where they should be. All is ready. The protective plastic cover is rolled back from the catwalk; the lights dim over the audience and blaze forth above the runway as the music begins.

Suddenly, all the hassle, all the frustration, all the discomfort seems a small price to pay for the privilege of being first to view the maestro's new clothes. Even the poor Japanese, almost always given the worst seats in the auditorium, enjoy it. A good fashion show is theatre; it is circus; it is dance; above all, it is glamour. And that is why everyone fights to get in; that is why journalists – for all their moans – would hate to be treated like professionals, as Armani tried to do. They do not want information in a logical and rational form; they do not care about handling materials and touching garments. What they want is light, noise, movement and, above all, involvement with a theatrical spectacle. Hit me, punch me, spit on me, degrade me in whatever way you will, they sob, but please, please don't leave me out.

8

Supplement Living

The catalyst for fashion change is discontent. Too often we are convinced that the only remedy for feelings of social uncertainty or insecurity about our sexuality is a change of clothes. This is an illusion that the fascistic nature of the fashion business is keen to exploit.

The media spent the first years of the new decade informing us that there has been a change of attitude, a new emphasis that makes us disgusted with the excesses of the Eighties. But consumerism still sells newspapers and magazines. Every Sunday we are drenched by a shower of style and fashion; we are told what to wear on every day of the week by tabloids and broadsheets alike. Magazines – struggling in the grip of a freeze on advertising revenue – have changed tack but not altered the message. We must be made to continue buying. In the 1980s when Liz Tilberis – than editor of British *Vogue* – was asked about the high prices of clothes featured in her magazine, she replied, 'You cannot ask the editor of *Vogue* about prices.' New voices speak for the 1990s. Justifying her decision to devote an issue of *Vogue* to secondary, cheaper diffusion lines, current editor Alexandra Shulman told the *Sunday Times*, '*Vogue* has always reflected its time; to ignore prices would be philistine.'

The observers and experts who interpret the world of high fashion for the rest of us have a duty to warn us off wasting our money on garments which are anything but top quality in conception, workmanship and appearance. But they do not do so because they know that to deaden our desire is to destroy themselves.

A critic must have a perspective of time if what he says is to be of any value. Who would respect commentary on Andy Warhol from a man who did not understand what makes Rembrandt superior? What credibility would a theatre critic command who had read Tom Stoppard but not Shakespeare? And yet fashion writers, with very few exceptions, are in exactly that situation. It is not entirely their fault. Although Warhol's approach to art is far removed from the easel painting of Rembrandt, they can both be assessed using the same criteria. Even though Stoppard's stagecraft is vastly different from that of Shakespeare, the same rules of communication still apply. Fashion lacks this continuum. Being a practical thing – despite the frivolity and extravagance – it responds to developments in all areas of life, not least those of personal prestige, locomotion and decency. A villain from Shakespeare's time is not much different from a villain in a Stoppard play, but the vast changes that have occurred in dress, even over a period as brief as the last hundred years, make it extremely difficult for fashion commentators to find any common ground between clothing then and today.

Fashion journalists live permanently in the present. But there are the 'quality' writers who have read about Schiaparelli and Chanel and recognise the names of Molyneux and Mainbocher although they could not necessarily distinguish one designer's creations from another. This is the equivalent in the art world of not being able to tell a Tiepolo sketch from one by Gainsborough, or of knowing that Van Gogh was a post-Impressionist, but being unable to see any difference between his work and Cezanne's. Such ignorance would be unacceptable in someone paid to comment and inform with authority.

Many couturiers have little but contempt for the press corps; many more are bewildered by it. How many times have I heard the cry, 'But Colin, they know *nothing*! Absolutely *nothing*!' It is a cry reserved most frequently for British and American journalists. A designer's heart sinks when someone under the age of 30 is wheeled in to interview him because, rightly or wrongly, he assumes that any references he may make to earlier designers, let alone his country's cultural history, will be met with blank incomprehension. I remember two agonised comments. 'If they do not understand Balenciaga and Fath,' a French couturier once asked, 'how can they hope to assess me?' Another comment, from an Italian: 'I talk of Walter Albini – one of the founding fathers of Italian fashion – *molto importante* – who only died in 1983 and they have never heard of him!'

There are good reasons why so much ignorance exists in the fashion world. It is harder to see examples of the great dresses of the twentieth century than to see great paintings. Dresses are delicate, vulnerable things. They fade, they tear, they lose their embroidery, their silver and gold become tarnished but, worst of all, they are often considered by their owners as adaptable in a way a painting never is. Only a psychopath would cut an inch off a Monet to make it fit a modern frame, but many women would not think twice about doing the same thing to a Poiret in order to make it fit their figure or the fashion mood of the time. Even where dresses do survive intact, museums must preserve them. Over half the dresses by the major designers kept in costume collections such as those of the Victoria and Albert Museum in London or New York's Metropolitan Museum of Art are in storage, and those that are on display may not be touched or handled. They languish behind glass in subdued light, looking nothing more than sad. This is all right and proper. Delicate old materials are vulnerable. But it does raise the question of how young journalists are to learn about the history of fashion in practical terms in order to fit themselves to be critics rather than mere reactors to, or publicists of, the current mode.

In most major cities there are libraries that contain copies of fashion magazines. A good municipal or college library is likely to have back issues of *Vogue*, *L'Officiel* or *Jardin des Modes*. Such publications are an invaluable source of training for the fashion journalist. Most of the great garments of the world have been photographed by them and, equally valuable, so have the lesser – the adaptations, the versions made to a price for a high street market. As recently as the 1960s, these clothes were photographed in a way that not only showed the essence of the design but exemplified the spirit of the age in which they were created. The last twenty-five years, however, have seen a change of emphasis in fashion photography. Editors of glossy magazines no longer see as necessary the depiction of clothes in a way that makes clear their design: the spirit of the age in a modern fashion photograph is often considered more important than the essence of the design. Frequently the result is fashion magazines which are more like photographic magazines – of little use for shaping the future of the art of dress design or reporting.

The changes in the nature of fashion publications and news-papers also discourage serious commentary. In the past, they had a practical content. Not all women who wished to dress well could afford the creations of the great couturiers, or even the line-for-line copies made, with the couturier's approval, by the dressmaking and tailoring departments of stores like New York's Henri Bendel or Harrods of London. For such a woman, a picture in a magazine, whether a drawing or a photograph, was important. Of equal value was the informed and descriptive writing of a professional journalist.

Succinct and informative, such writing had a real purpose: to convey information to the millions of women who had their clothes made for them on the principles laid down by Paris, so that they could pass this on to local dressmakers and tailors who needed to know as clearly as possible what the season's mode was to be. This need gave fashion journalism an edge and immediacy which no longer exists in modern fashion writing. What couturiers propose in ready-to-wear is a full season ahead of its realisation. It will be filtered, tamed or, if necessary, enlivened by the ready-to-wear designers who bring fashion to the high street. Whatever is shown on the catwalk at the couturier's fashion shows is modified to make it acceptable for sale in the shops. There are few private dressmakers left to interpret the Paris line for individual customers. So the insistence on precise and informed writing about fashion has disappeared, and the gap is filled by the broadsheets with sociological babble. The tabloids turn fashion into sexual fantasy.

When, rightly or wrongly, fashion was seen as a minor but vital part of the arts – as it was in the 1920s, 1930s and even up to the 1950s – it attracted not only artists but also the same considered attention that art was given in newspapers and journals. Intellectuals found nothing inconsistent in attending a fashion show, which was not seen as an exclusively female occasion. As Colette wrote in *Vogue* in the Thirties, a man could feel 'entirely at his ease . . . at the dress shows he will meet the painter of the moment, the smart socialite and her novelist, the politician and his Egeria.' Cocteau could be found in the front row at Chanel, Gertrude Stein at Balmain, Sartre at Dior. Writers of the calibre of Truman Capote, André Maurois and Paul Gallico were happy to accept commissions from *Vogue* and *Harper's Bazaar*. Although it can be argued that in those days *Vogue* and *Harper's Bazaar* were society magazines as much as fashion magazines, the point remains that fashion was part of the intellectual whole in which intelligent, educated, cultured people of both sexes could be expected to take some interest. Such people required writing on fashion as informed and informative as writing on literature, art, music and the social scene.

When couture was pushed aside in the late 1950s, the importance of fashion was severely diminished. As the swinging

Sixties developed, it was reduced to the level of home dressmaking or the most primitive tailoring techniques. All intellectual interest evaporated. Ready-to-wear fashion required no informed criticism. Fashion became permanently severed from the rest of the arts. And so it has remained.

Many fashion journalists believe that fashion history began with Biba and Mary Quant. I recall talking to one about a book she hoped to write. 'I want it be be historic,' she said. 'To go right back.' 'How far?' I enquired. 'Oh, the Fifties.' 'The 1850s?' 'No, the 1950s, to get all the history and that.'

When Suzy Menkes arrives at her hotel in Milan to cover the Italian ready-to-wear shows, she can hardly find a place to unpack her case, so full is her room of flowers, fruit and enticingly glossy shopping bags bearing the names of the top-runners in the Italian fashion world. Orchids, freesias, lilies, wild woodland plants and violets fill every available space. Each arrangement is exquisite. Crowding what little space is left are bowls and baskets of perfect fruit – grapes sparkling with beads of water; tiny exotic fruits from almost inaccessible corners of the tropical world and, snuggling in the middle of this cornucopia, a bottle of the best champagne – or, even greater privilege, a fine wine from a private vineyard. The sort of gift that a recipient would savour for days, if not weeks.

Then there are the bags containing the latest perfume from one of the great masters of Italian fashion, maybe a beautiful crocodile-skin diary, with matching crocodile and silver pen; perhaps a scarf of thick, creamy silk with hand-rolled hems; even, on occasion, a leather handbag bearing the initials that personify sophistication to the whole world.

This welcome for Suzy Menkes is not unique. It is shared by many other key fashion journalists, and is a mark of how highly they are respected – although only in fashion does respect for one's professional talents lead inevitably to increased, though tacit, attempts at bribery. The munificence of the maestros is in direct proportion to the importance of the newspapers or journals that Suzy and her fellow writers represent. Suzy Menkes is wise in the ways of fashion houses. She knows that were she to leave the *International Herald Tribune* suddenly, she would have absolutely no difficulty in finding space to unpack.

Not as inventive as Paris, less outrageous than London, and totally lacking the laid-back ease of New York design, Milan's fashion gurus have sometimes wondered where their niche actually falls in world terms. To cover their uncertainty they have resorted to what is little more than bribery. It is hard for a journalist wearing a silk blouse accepted as a gift to write critically of the collection of the donor. And, as they also know, most journalists find it even harder to return the parcel unopened.

Milan has always been more generous in the gift business than the other centres of fashion. London designers never could afford expensive gifts, but that did not matter in the Eighties because they were able to trot out the world's two most famous women in order to silence criticism. An invitation to meet Mrs Thatcher at No. 10 or curtsy to the Princess of Wales at Kensington Palace was irresistible, even to American journalists brought up in a culture of egalitarianism. Couturiers in Paris, knowing that the world is afraid of them, find that their very arrogance is sufficient to keep journalists in awe although some, like Karl Lagerfeld, will send little welcoming gifts to hotels for the *crème de la crème* of journalists, simply because it amuses him.

In New York, foreign journalists are rated lower than the front-liners of the American press. Gifts, if any, have always been 'token' and a reward for turning up for the show rather than an attempt to influence copy – a phial of eau de toilette (never the full-strength and costly *parfum*); a cotton T-shirt or, in the case of Calvin Klein, a cotton bathrobe emblazoned with his name.

In the 1990s this downbeat approach has become the norm. Whereas the front-row gals like Suzy still get flowers, their hotel rooms no longer resemble the hothouse at Kew and, for the majority, the gifts are low key, non-embarrassing and, it must be said, low cost, to fit in with the new financial stringency.

At the celebrations for Dunhill's 100th anniversary in London in early 1993, press ladies pursed lips when they discovered that the 'goodie' bags contained nothing more exotic than three Dunhill handkerchiefs – cotton, at that. But the ways of the Eighties cannot be sustained in the Nineties; for cashmere and silk now read lambswool and cotton. The most magnificently inappropriate gift for women haunted by the fear of putting on an ounce is the perfectly packaged box of chocolates – all hand-dipped, of course – which goes immediately to mothers, aunts or the typing pool. The most coveted are the toiletries – they make such marvellously prestigious Christmas presents or gifts for hostesses of country weekends – which are packaged to the highest level of sophistication. A couple of seasons ago, Armani gave top journalists a range of toiletries wrapped in a green and white striped cotton material rather like interfacing. Imagine the surprise for the sophisticated Milanese when foreign journalists – mainly English and German – began to wear them as scarves in order to show that they 'rated' a gift from Armani.

The wearable gift has been reduced to the definitely non-status T-shirt, which, even emblazoned with the designer's name, no fashion journalist who has any belief in her status would dream of wearing in Milan, Paris or New York. In the past, a scarf casually tied, a cashmere wrap nonchalantly assumed, even a pair of Chanel earrings, made clear who was – and, more importantly, who was *not* – rated by the designers.

Standards must be lax in a profession that allows its employees to take so much advantage of freebies. Some papers have forbidden their journalists to do so. But most do not bother, and the reason editors can get away with it is that they treat fashion very much as a sideshow. Objective criticism has little interest for them

145

or their readers and the designers want quantity of coverage, not quality.

In the late 1980s the fashion editors of broadsheets learned that they could please designers by getting a picture on the front or first two pages of their newspapers whilst, at the same time, giving editors and picture editors a *frisson* of excitement because they felt that they were being 'sexy'. The tabloids responded aggressively to this poaching of their preserve by publishing bigger and sexier pictures than they had before. The designers quickly cottoned on. It became a cliché of the late 1980s and early 1990s that every collection had to have a '*Sun*' dress which was revealing, lace-trimmed and usually satin, and which bore absolutely no relationship to the designer's true fashion philosophy. Journalists grew used to being dazzled by the cameramen's flashguns when such a dress appeared on the runway.

As even luxury trades began to be affected by the world depression, hitherto sober designers made increasing numbers of '*Sun*' dresses in an attempt to hog the newspaper fashion pages. The more desperate began to produce whole collections with an emphasis on the sleazier aspects of sexy dressing. Newspaper editors went wild; fashion editors bowed to the inevitable and designers of the calibre of Gianni Versace became household names. The influence of the '*Sun*' approach to fashion journalism has been dire and its effect on fashion catastrophic.

Most newspaper editors and art editors are male. They do not have to wear the dresses they feature. Most women who buy dresses do so in the realisation that the demands of taste, expediency and (in these days when violence against women is increasing) even safety preclude the sort of revealing dress that newspaper men love so much. They reject the attitude as vigorously as they reject the clothes, as demonstrated in 1993 by the violent reaction to the suggestion by Conrad Black, proprietor of the *Daily Telegraph*, that, because he considered his wife's legs sexy, designers should be booed for trying to scupper the mini-skirt.

Any newspaper editor aware of sales and advertising revenue knows that a good fashion picture presents a visual talking point even if it is only of the 'I wouldn't be seen dead in *that*' variety. The words are much more problematic. How many readers really want the sociopolitical commentary that some broadsheets see as obligatory in order to justify the inclusion on their pages of anything so 'frivolous' as frocks? How many care about the warmed-over news stories from *Women's Wear Daily* which are the standard fare of at least one London fashion journalist?

No one seems to know where fashion is going, and the answer will not come from the British fashion press. Again, the males who run the media are largely to blame. When the waters become muddied, experience and knowledge are required. But London's newspaper editors, notoriously sexist, are also ageist: they believe that fashion can only be understood and written about by the young, who are supposed to have drive and flair, and to be iconoclastic. In an attempt to prove that they are also forever young, editors enjoy appearing at London's rare fashion bashes on the arms of pretty young fashion editors who look the part even if they know little about their subject.

Fashion writers still in their forties are removed from jobs; their applications for senior posts are passed over. Instead, women in their late twenties and early thirties are considered to have better legs and firmer breasts and therefore to be more suitable. Aware that 'image' reflects on them within their own world, newspaper editors desire the approbation of their kind rather than taking account of the needs of their readers who will, perhaps, never see the fashion writer in person and will judge her, the newspaper and its editor by her words alone.

Suzy Menkes, for example, is on what editors would consider the wrong side of 40. Married with a grown-up family, she is the antithesis of the 'bimbo' fashion editor, bringing the experience of more than twenty years' reporting fashion to every piece she writes. And yet every opportunity is taken to sneer at her appearance and mannerisms. Why is this? Why should a mild-mannered, hard-working professional at the pinnacle of her career be so treated? She is laughed at by younger women frightened of her achievements which they know they cannot emulate; younger women who can only face their ignorance by denigrating her knowledge; younger women who draw the parameters of their self-esteem with the chalk of their youth.

In America, they order things differently. Fashion journalists on major newspapers or syndicated coast-to-coast are expected to be mature – just as theatre critics, art historians and literary commentators are. The doyennes of American fashion – Bernadine Morris of the *New York Times*, Mary Lou Luther of the *Los Angeles Times* Syndicate and Nina Hyde of the *Washington Post* – are not young, but that does not mean they should bow their heads for the chopping block. They flourish, knowing that their most valuable asset is the age which brings the knowledge that US editors are keen to buy.

Consider Carrie Donovan recently of the *NYT Magazine*, respected, even revered, at the age of 55. A graduate of Parsons School of Design, she worked briefly as a designer in the Fifties before becoming a journalist for the *New York Times*. From there, she moved to *Vogue*, on to *Harper's Bazaar* and back to the *Times*. Donovan is wooed and cosseted simply because of the time it has taken to amass so much experience. She was described in the pages of American *Vogue* as an 'old, marvelous glam fashion lady' and no one felt any credibility gap between the adjectives.

The world's most famous magazine editors are all British: Tina Brown, Liz Tilberis and Anna Wintour bestride Manhattan Island. This, however, raises a new question. Isn't their presence a permanent insult to American journalists? Tilberis and Wintour can be seen as the beneficiaries of the Brown fallout – for she was the one whose success with *Vanity Fair* initially gave American publishers confidence in London talent – and they are obligingly continuing the 'think Brit' movement, surrounding themselves with old colleagues and accents they can *trust*. It is a growing list: Georgina Howell on American *Vogue* is followed by Hamish Bowles, who is followed by Suzy Menkes (on a freelance basis); Sarah Mower on *Harper's Bazaar* is replaced while on maternity leave by Sally Brampton, ex-editor of British *Elle*. Is this chauvinism of the narrowest kind, or is it fear? Do Wintour and Tilberis treat US talent with contempt or is it part of normal British arrogance to assume that our journalists can communicate with North Americans better than the home-grown variety can? Are there no good fashion journalists in the US?

Of course there are. And some of the new Brits in New York, experienced knockabout journalists though they might be, are hardly exceptional as writers or fashion commentators. I recall leaving a Gianfranco Ferre show of startling technical brilliance a few years ago and asking one of them if she had enjoyed it. 'Horrible, I would not wear any of it,' she replied. Ferre's clothes at that time were all about drop-dead, high-class sexuality – towering heels, short skirts, deep cleavage – which British journalists all seem to distrust. I turned to the stylist Debbi Mason, whose philosophy of fashion could not be more different. 'It was marvellous,' she said. 'Brilliant tailoring. A *tour de force*.' 'Would you wear any of it?' I asked. Debbi looked puzzled. 'No,' she said. 'But that has nothing to do with it. Ferre is a genius. That's the point, even though I do not like how he views women.'

Anna Wintour's career in editing has been meteoric, since her first job in 1970 with British *Harper's Bazaar*, which at that time had not amalgamated with *Queen* to become *Harpers & Queen*. Her New York connection began in 1976 when she joined American *Harper's Bazaar*, edited then – and, indeed, until ousted in 1992 by Tilberis – by Tony Mazzola, a long-term stalwart of Hearst Publications. Feeling that she did not understand the US market, he sacked Wintour, who went on to make a great success of the job of fashion editor of *New York* magazine before moving to American *Vogue* in 1983 as 'creative director'. When Beatrice Miller retired as editor of British *Vogue*, Wintour was the obvious choice of successor. After initial hesitation, she accepted the post.

What happened to Anna Wintour in London is yet another example of our worst characteristic – chauvinism. Although her father was British, Wintour was tarred with the US brush. The fashion press viewed her not only as an interloper but also – in a strange rehearsal for what Wintour was later to do to American journalists – as an insult to senior fashion journalists of British nationality who had not enjoyed the high life of Manhattan, as it was imagined Anna Wintour had. So all the paranoia of British fashion journalists began to surface: the sentimentality about being British and 'sticking in' even when life is difficult; puritanism of the kind that criticised GI brides for escaping post-war austerity; jealousy – Anna Wintour was so much more elegant, slim and fashionable than all but a handful of British fashion journalists. Above all, what made Anna Wintour so unpopular was her naked ambition, and the fact that she was a real worker. Wintour did not wish to sit over lunch until 3.30, and then arrive back at the office, as many of her peers did, awash with alcohol and rich food. She appeared to be that most unnatural of all creatures in the fashion world – a puritan.

Anna Wintour's dedication, and her clear belief in what she felt a fashion magazine for the Eighties should be saying, destroyed the image that Miller had built up for *Vogue*. The slightly eccentric, fantasy quality was elbowed aside. Clothes for real lives were photographed not on dreamy girls in meadows but on models leaping off pavements and running for buses. British *Vogue* stopped being impossibly aristocratic and became mildly sexy.

London was shocked. When Wintour returned to New York to edit the US edition of *House and Garden*, eyes remained dry. Eager to make her mark again in New York, Wintour revamped *House and Garden*, leaving traditional readers bewildered. She renamed it *HG*, caused a great stir and, eight issues later, received the glittering prize – Grace Mirabella was removed from American *Vogue* and editorship of the world's most powerful magazine was Wintour's. *HG* was buried in 1993. To London's great surprise, Liz Tilberis took over British *Vogue*.

She stayed there only briefly. Less than happy with the Condé Nast management, she was reported to be at loggerheads with managing director Nicholas Coleridge. According to the *Daily Express*, she criticised the firm's 'schoolboy management', although she has since denied doing so. Clearly ill at ease in her London role, she finally accepted the inducements of the Hearst Organization and became editor designate of *Harper's Bazaar*.

Harper's Bazaar had, at one time, been America's most avant-garde fashion magazine. With Carmel Snow as editor, Vreeland as fashion editor and Alexey Brodovitch as art editor, it was a trailblazer in the 1950s but, after Brodovitch's resignation in 1958 and Vreeland's defection to *Vogue* in 1962, the magazine had steadily gone downhill, losing ground to *Vogue* in prestige, readership figures and, most important of all, advertising revenue. By 1987 a crisis had been reached, as the advertising figures show. *Vogue*'s revenue from advertising was $79.5 million, *Harper's* $32.5 million. Further, the two traditional sparring partners had been joined by a third – the US edition of *Elle*, which was making an impact that worried both. It booked $39 million of advertising in 1987 and, selling 850,000 copies per month, had quickly overtaken *Harper's Bazaar*, whose ad pages had fallen almost 11 per cent by 1988.

Liz Tilberis's first issue – September 1992 – was sensationally different from Wintour's *Vogue* and was hailed as bringing an element of European class to fashion magazines in America. It did no such thing. What Tilberis and her creative director, Fabien Baron, had done was much simpler – and much closer to home. They went back thirty years to the days of Vreeland and Brodovitch and produced a pastiche of their pages. The typography and use of white space were direct rip-offs of the Brodovitch style, although, in my opinion, the work of photographers like Patrick Demarchelier lagged a long way behind that of Vreeland's star photographer, Richard Avedon. The trademark white background of Tilberis's covers tells the tale: this is a cool magazine for sophisticates, in the grand manner of the Fifties fashion publications.

Wintour's *Vogue* is altogether jollier. From its sassy, bimbo cover girls to its busy editorial pages, American *Vogue* has a downmarket, populist appeal. If Wintour likes something or feels that it represents the mood of the moment, she assumes that her readers need to be banged over the head with it. If a top hat appears in one fashion photograph, it is likely to appear in ten; she themes her pages so successfully that the magazine becomes a primer, a grammar of what to wear, what to eat, what to think and what to see. In this, she also follows the Vreeland line – with much the same success, although none of the class. American readers do not like irony; they are uneasy if an approach is oblique; they like to be led. This is something Wintour understands and Tilberis has still to learn.

Anna Wintour has a head start, of course. She has much the greater experience as an American editor and knows the US fashion world extremely well. But, as one of Liz Tilberis's colleagues told me, 'Liz may look like a cosy Labrador, but she is a Rottweiler. She never gives up and is never beaten.' And she has certainly pulled off some amazing 'firsts', not least her spectacular coup in persuading the Princess of Wales to be photographed by Demarchelier for a cover of British *Vogue*. The picture made her look so like a fashion model that it was clear she had missed her true vocation by marrying into the royal family.

Tilberis and Wintour are locked in a deadly battle for a dwindling US readership. How much influence either will have on the way American women view fashion and, indeed, themselves, it is too early to say. What is certain is that they have much competition from rival magazines like *Elle*, *Mirabella* – founded by Grace Mirabella after leaving *Vogue* – and a host of less exalted titles. In particular, neither of them has matched the power of the Fairchild Organization, which publishes the daily newspaper *Women's Wear Daily*, bible of the US fashion world, and *W*, its social and fashion magazine that is crammed full of luxury advertising for jewellery, watches, perfumes and make-up. The European version – a perfect-bound fashion magazine called *W Fashion Europe* – is already beginning to attract readers away from the more well-established European titles, although it is only three years old. This is good news for John Fairchild, in whose stable of fashion publications it is becoming a star.

Fairchild is not an editor, but he is certainly a power. His name is well known to people who have only vaguely heard of Bernard Leser, president of Condé Nast Publications, or S. I. Newhouse, its owner, and have never heard of D. Claeys Bahrenburg, president of Hearst Magazines. Fairchild is a high-profile fashion front-liner who has linked the prestige of his publications to his personal power rating in the fashion world. Who has ever heard of a Fairchild editor? Who rates an individual fashion editor from his stable? Nobody – and the reason is simple. John Fairchild believes in keeping to himself both the power and the glory. All major decisions appear to be his. The job of the editorial staff is to implement those decisions.

John Fairchild rightly sees himself as a king-maker – *WWD* is feared by Seventh Avenue and by every US designer. It is the most powerful publication in the fashion world. *Ipso facto*, John Fairchild is the most powerful individual in that world.

Fairchild publications outshine all the rest. *Women's Wear Daily*'s reports on the international collections are vital reading for anyone seriously interested in fashion, as are its in-depth investigations of the industry and its personality pieces on designers. For all their quality if every copy of *Vogue* and *Harper's Bazaar* for the last ten years, along with all other fashion magazines published throughout the world, were destroyed in some holocaust, provided *WWD* was saved, their loss would hardly be noticed by the industry. It is thanks to the genius of John Fairchild – capricious, arbitrary and destructive as it can be – that the fashion industry has such a decisive and authentic organ to help it be taken seriously by governments, financiers and business organisations. In comparison with *WWD* other publications are little more than pretty picture-books of clothes.

In commercial terms, there is no reason why they should be otherwise. Fashion magazines exist not as archives for posterity but as here-and-now vehicles to attract advertising revenue. For this, they need not only the right number but also the right type of readers. That is why they proudly publish reader profiles – their ABC rating. If they can claim a high number of A and B readers, classified at the top of the social tree as having the best education, social standing and, above all, buying power of the population, then they will attract the top advertisers and be able to charge them the highest rates. The formula is simple. Readers of British *Vogue* and any other luxury magazine are assumed to buy items which they see in the editorial pages – which is why prices and stockists of featured merchandise are always shown, with the exception of top-quality designer clothing or items from *haute couture* ranges where the prices are so high as to be laughable.

How many women actually buy merchandise featured in British *Vogue* and usually, but not always, priced at the higher end of the market, is not easily discovered. The vast majority of high street shoppers rarely, if ever, see a copy of the magazine. Paradoxically, however, this does not diminish *Vogue*'s influence on high street fashion, which is more powerful than that of any other British magazine. '*Vogue*' has become almost a generic term for high fashion, quality and class. When the editorial pages feature merchandise from fashion chains or department stores, retailers proudly display the pictures, backed by the slogan, 'As Seen in *Vogue*'. They pay Condé Nast for this, of course, but they do so willingly, knowing that the magic name of *Vogue* will give the product a cachet that guarantees sales. Other magazines use the same device to make money from their editorial pages, but 'As Seen in *Elle*, *Tatler*, *Harpers & Queen*, *Woman's Journal et al.*' simply does not have the ring of quality and, even more importantly, the incontrovertible fashion authority encapsulated in the word '*Vogue*'.

British *Vogue*'s influence on what ordinary women buy and wear is real, despite the fact that relating to the editorial pages is almost impossible for most of them. It is, quite simply, the magazine that all other publications watch – and copy. The message that is picked up is nothing to do with the commentary and everything to do with the photography. *Vogue* stylists have enormous influence. The world is literally theirs. If Nicholas Coleridge was right about the madness of fashion editors, it is as nothing compared with the craziness of high fashion stylists.

I have seen photographers despairingly untying scarves, removing decorations from hair and tossing aside jewellery in a bid for the simplicity that enables them to capture the essence of a garment. Stylists *loathe* simplicity because it makes their work redundant. They scour the exotic art, the ethnic and decoration books in Hatchards, for ideas to justify expensive shoots in exotic parts of the world. Nevertheless, the *Vogue* approach to fashion permeates the market and eventually reaches the mass readership publications which cater for women with slim budgets and large figures. The magazine's advertising pages are less perfect than the editorial section of the magazine and therefore more easily related to. Advertising in *Vogue* is costly – up to £25,000 for a double-page spread. But manufacturers and designers consider it worthwhile, not merely because of the potential sales to individual women but also because it is important to show confidence to the middle men – the stockists, manufacturers and suppliers.

Fashion PRs are even more powerful in perpetuating the designer scam than the most self-seeking of journalists. Their influence within the industry is immense and yet they rarely or never have to justify their actions to the public. They are the court clerics of fashion, who move from group to group, influencing, cajoling and even intimidating in order to obtain their way. Their main role in fashion is to keep the product of the accounts for whom they work in the public eye. Profile is all.

Although the world's very successful designers prefer to employ their own in-house PRs because they are usually so paranoid about their clothes and image, there are plenty of others who will pay handsomely for an independent PR firm. An annual fee of £50,000 would not be considered out of the way in London. Most successful PR firms acquire at least five major accounts quite apart from several minor ones, and after overheads (most of which are billed to the client anyway), considerable amounts of money are made in this strange fashion by-way.

Beneath the cut-glass accents lurk cut-throat attitudes, as PR firms fight for each other's accounts and push their clients' claims. The PR job is to get the story on the page and, in order to do so, they are always aware of the latest diversion with which to titillate the ladies. Bored with the Ivy? Tired of Le Caprice's salmon fish cakes? Can't stand the noise at Quaglino's? A new and even more fashionable spot will be found for launch. Then there are the favourites – Orso, Daphne's, the Greenhouse, Mosimann's. Even though the bill will be outrageous, it is worth it. It is pleasant for the PR to lunch in such places, it flatters the journalist, and it feeds the self-esteem of the client to see so much of his money being spent in such posh places. Shows he's got class. No hole-in-the-wall, Dirty Dick diner for our company, thank you very much. This is, after all, probably the only business where you risk losing a job if you do not spend enough money.

Like whores loitering behind the trenches, PRs are not really part of the front-line battle. Theirs is a service industry on a *Kiss of the Spiderwoman* scale. First the victim is selected. Any PR worth her salt has a personal stable of tame journalists – friends, darling – whom she has cosseted to such an extent that they will take any story, push any product when the time comes to 'call in' the free lunches . . . and samples conveniently not asked to be returned . . . and Christmas presents . . . and promotional trips to exotic lands. Lapland for a perfume lunch? Marvellous, darling, I'll be there.

Then comes the enmeshing. The lunch. The theatre trip. The gala night at the ballet. And, again, the jaunt abroad.

To understand the lure of the jaunt it is important to remember how many journalists are unattached. When the glamour party stops, they will return to frequently lonely and very unexotic flats for a cup of Nescafé and a quick look at *News at Ten*. Experienced as they are in travel, they find it hard to holiday alone. PRs know this and that is why they can usually persuade clients to foot the bill for what, for many journalists, is a holiday with all the advantages. A famous London PR – one of the doyennes of her trade – once took a group of journalists to New Mexico to promote a beauty range. It soon became apparent that the trip was in danger of being ruined if one edgy journalist could not be made to relax. Showing the mettle that took her to the top of her profession, our PR came up with a solution. Secret consultations with management, an exchange of money and suddenly two young Mexicans appeared to entertain the journalist on a shift system. All tension disappeared. As the PR confessed, 'It was an expenditure not budgeted for, but it was money well spent.'

The basic job of most PR firms could be done more efficiently and infinitely more cheaply by a good courier service and mail-shot company. What has made PR women essential to the industry is the role they have carved out as corrupters who truss up their prey so cunningly that there is barely a fashion journalist immune to their power. Their siren call lures journalists to lunch wherever they propose, except for those on *Vogue*, known as the Condé Nastites or even Condé Nasties, who exploit *their* power and bid the PRs to come to them, preferring to eat in their own demesne at the fashionable Italian trat, O'Keefe's, just down the road from Vogue House. In the power battleground of the public relations world all things are possible and nothing carved in stone. Getting that all-important picture or those vital words in the right place at the right time justifies anything that has to be done.

9

Bulletins from the Asylum

'Twenty years ago they were still trade persons . . . .They should all be happy that people pay them so much attention. After rock stars and a few movie stars . . . they make more money than anybody else.' Karl Lagerfeld (who often seems to me to be the only designer who ever says anything worth saying) considers that his contemporaries take themselves too seriously.

Traditionally, dress designers have viewed their creations with a pretentious eye. For them, they are not merely clothes. They are an artistic statement, an experience, the fruit of six months of intensive, creative slog. Rose Bertin, generally considered the first dressmaker sufficiently important to be remembered by name, was *marchande de modes* to Marie Antoinette and the court of Versailles. A firm favourite of the Queen, who even broke with protocol to allow her *modiste* – who was not of noble blood – to be present at the *levée* in order to help her dress, Rose Bertin felt that she could snub or patronise any member of the aristocracy who in her opinion did not live up to the Queen's standards of elegance in dress. When Marie Antoinette went to the guillotine, Bertin's head metaphorically was also chopped off. There were no more customers for beautiful clothes, created to be cast aside within a month; no more demand for outrageous headwear concocted to express the mood of the moment and discarded within the week; no more frivolous occasions when a courtier's sartorial standing could be ruined by the gossip of an hour. The French Revolution exposed Rose Bertin's posturing as utterly frivolous – and as short-lived as the reputations of most of her dressmaking contemporaries.

But there were others to carry forward the flame of pretension. Most famous – and arrogant – of all was the man credited with founding modern couture: Charles Frederick Worth, an Englishman who went to work in Paris in 1845. He transformed the old dressmaking business to found what was, in effect, a completely new trade – that of couturier, a man who did not act on instructions from customers but made proposals (that is, designed clothes consulting only his muse) for them to accept. No backsliding was permitted, no questioning of the maestro's wishes allowed. Riding on royal backs as Bertin had, Worth made no concessions to the whims of his clients and, as his association with the Empress Eugénie and all the crowned heads of Europe grew more secure, his posturing became the scandal of Paris. Customers were expected to make an appointment with him, regardless of rank or title – an unheard-of thing with a dressmaker. Given a number, rather in the manner of a supermarket delicatessen, women were made to wait until their moment to meet the maestro arrived. Such behaviour from a tradesman in the second half of the nineteenth century was outrageous, but it was accepted.

Worth must be credited with single-handedly changing the status of his calling so that a top couturier was never again to be seen as a mere trader. Like a portrait painter, architect or interior decorator, he became equal to his customers and worthy of their respect, regardless of his background, because of his knowledge and skill and the fact that he was contributing to the power of the woman whose patronage of him he was also patronising. Worth got away with all his nonsense because the fashionable world convinced itself that, having been chosen by the Empress, he must be not only the best but the very nonpareil of a dressmaker. It is a form of indoctrination that still works today where there are few absolute standards and designers are only as good as fashionable arbiters believe they are. Not that Worth's antics passed without critical comment: Hippolyte Taine viciously satirised him and Charles Dickens viewed him with a coolly appraising eye. Their opinions had no effect, apart from making him even better known. Fashionable society was as indifferent to the comments of intellectuals as it it today, and Worth continued in the ascendant as a social and artistic power in the land.

What he did for Paris and couture cannot be overestimated. The arrogant, wilful couturier has become a lasting part of fashion folklore – the man, or woman, who demands respect, even adulation, for that magic moment when the new creations are shown to the world.

Paul Poiret, who followed Worth chronologically as well as spiritually, once cut down to size the Countess Greffulhe, model for Proust's Duchess de Guermantes in *A la Recherche du temps perdu*, by asking during a fitting if her comment that the dress she was trying on made her look like a Greek column meant that she was complaining. 'No,' she replied, 'I am well satisfied. That is what counts, is it not?' 'No,' Poiret said. '*I* am satisfied, and *that* is what counts.'

Chanel . . . Patou . . . Schiaparelli . . . the grand couturiers of the century all played the power game with customers and press (Chanel and Patou quarrelled bitterly with *Vogue* whenever the editor dared to place their models on facing pages), knowing that the more arrogant and aloof they appeared, the more desirable they became. As part of the personality cult, the idea evolved that the couturier would remain hidden during the show so that he might be coaxed unwillingly out at the end in response to the applause. It is a charade carried on even today in the rough-and-tumble world of the ready-to-wear shows. Model girls dragging on to the catwalk designers who pretend that such exposure is the last thing they want is a cliché of our times, contrasting sharply with the assurance of Chanel, who was sufficiently confident in her organisation to allow backstage to look after itself as she sat at the top of the stairs in rue Cambon watching not her clothes but her audience's reaction; or Balenciaga, so elusive and exclusive that even regular customers rarely saw him, who watched the audience through a curtain and made a mental note of those whose attention wavered.

It is part of the hype inherent in the designer scam that today's megalomaniac couturier can unashamedly proclaim himself an artist without much fear of contradiction. It enables him to get away with murder. After all, the justification runs, was Mozart easy to live with or Picasso all sweetness and light? We must accept that great creators are frequently monsters.

For long periods of their existence, certain couturiers behave like madmen, petrified in case they cannot come up with ideas. Frequently the tension becomes too great. I have watched world-famous designers tear apart a dress in blind, impotent fury; roll on the floor in a foetal position and scream like a baby. I have heard the heartbreaking sob, 'If Balenciaga could do it, why can't we?' the desperate cry, 'I wish I were dead!'

At the heart of the couture house, the designer is shielded from the reality around him. His staff adore him and fulfil his demands without question; his business partner – an almost obligatory member of the entourage – is his public face, always ready to make excuses and tell as many barefaced lies as necessary.

If many of the great designers are vulnerable and insecure, even more are locked in an eternal childhood, passed from the adoring hands of over-protective mothers, determined to cosset their son's sensitivity against the harshness of the world, into the even more protective hands of the women who form an impenetrable carapace around him within the fashion house. It is with this Praetorian guard of women that the unreality begins. The air around them is heavy with menace, there is a miasma of nervousness, even fear, hanging over their perfectly coiffed heads that makes Proust's world seem as robust as an English Tourist Board commercial.

In the inner sanctum, all is silent and subdued. Unnaturally elegant, the women talk in whispers as they glide silently about their business; unhealthily pretty boys pass by bearing sketches as if entrusted with the Holy Grail itself. All sense of normality ebbs away as you wait – because it is an essential part of the mystique that you *always* have to wait. You become aware of the perfection of your surroundings. The flowers, which are almost always white, are so unblemished that, if you did not know better, you would be convinced they were made of silk – or even wax. The magazines on the side table are so precisely aligned it looks as though someone has measured their placing to a millimetre. You dare not touch them. You dare not touch anything. Your hands – and your feet, indeed every part of you – suddenly seem enormous, clodlike. The wait is having its effect. Your confidence cracks, as it is meant to.

But before you can make a dash for the door, a guide appears to take you deeper into this bizarre world. As you follow her, you are suddenly aware that she is the most unnerving thing about a great couture house. Perfectly dressed (always in black), immaculately made up, she seems like a warder, strong, determined and invulnerable. She acts like a strait-jacket for the lunatic caught at the centre of this web, the couturier himself, the victim of his own creation, his own success. Despite her confident appearance, however, this woman is gaunt with fear; her neck throbs with tension, her eyes twitch, her lips quiver. She is terrified of making a mistake.

It is a measure of the dedication – or hopelessness – of the midinettes and the myriad toilers who bolster the reputation of the designer that they accept the privations of the run-up to a collection without revolting. In a business where workers are notoriously badly paid and yet brought face to face with the huge wealth of others on a daily basis as they look around at the antique furniture, original paintings and the food and drink consumed on the other side of the sewing-room door, there is a devotion to the maestro that borders on fanaticism. I have known workers who began at 8 am still toiling at midnight, knowing that the next day – and the next – will be exactly the same. I have seen them at work for seven days a week for six weeks and more, and I have asked myself why. The answer is in the age-old reverence that the artisan has for the artist.

Their rewards may be slight in monetary terms but workroom heads, head fitters and tailors do, at least, enjoy the excitement of working literally at the cutting edge. Balenciaga, a stickler for perfection, cut and sewed alongside his workforce so often that they felt they had, if not an intimacy, certainly a spiritual understanding of 'Ba-ba', as they called him behind his back. Imagine how upset they were when the bombshell dropped. Balenciaga, most secretive of men, informed none of his staff when he closed his house in 1968. They only learned that their jobs had been whipped away through clients, the press and workers in other houses.

Balenciaga closed his doors with the words, 'It's a dog's life.' So it may be – but one lived in a gilded kennel. No designer worth his salt would dream of ordering a taxi himself, booking a table in a restaurant or knowing anything as banal as times of flights or even days of the week. Their energies, when they are not working on a collection, are channelled into a much more productive area – personal publicity.

It would be of great advantage to the health of fashion if criticism were more open. But employees are concerned to protect their employer, not attack him, and journalists are frightened of the retribution that can be meted out in return for a less than ecstatic reaction to a collection. It must not be forgotten that many dress designers are petulant, paranoid and petty. They can have a spirit of revenge that reduces the behaviour of the Borgias to the level of an Enid Blyton story.

Designers know, for example, that 'diverting' (a strong favourite in Italy) means a collection so disparate in ideas that it makes Don Quixote seem single-minded; 'droll' (beloved of the French) usually describes clothes that would have small boys splitting their sides with laughter and pointing in the streets were any woman unwise enough to wear them; 'signature' (used by everyone) implies that a designer is parading the same ideas he has shown endlessly in the last three seasons; 'essential' (a favourite with all nationalities) describes clothes so banal and unimaginative that they can be seen already on the streets; 'not as strong as last season' (another favourite) signals that the designer's gift to the journalist was in the wrong colour or too small; and 'fabulous' (used *ad nauseam*) can mean anything from the fact that the gift was just right and rather expensive to the simple response of one professional to another when in the presence of exquisitely wrought clothing.

Strange liaisons sometimes spring up between couturiers. Coco Chanel normally held the other designers in Paris in total contempt but she made an exception for Balenciaga, who gained her respect by his ability to cut and sew. Every collection he showed contained one discreet little black dress made entirely by the hand of the maestro but shown completely anonymously. As Chanel said, 'Only he is capable of cutting material, assembling a creation and sewing it by hand. The others are simply fashion designers.' She and Balenciaga visited Switzerland together, exchanged presents – Chanel gave him a portrait of herself painted by Cassandre – until, one day, things soured and they never spoke again.

For most couturiers, deadly combat with his rivals is the norm. But even a designer has to trust *someone*. Somebody has to handle meeting the public. Every designer I have ever met has a marvellous memory for names and rarely forgets a face, but they still need someone who will remember journalists and publications at show time, who can represent the 'personal' side of a business that long ago lost touch with the personal level. For this they rely on their in-house PR.

The PR is sandwiched between a demanding designer and a difficult public. It is no wonder that her face becomes hard, her string-thin body tense and her voice metallic. Although she fronts an industry renowned for taste and discretion, she knows that the slightest scratch across the surface will reveal the abattoir beneath. She is expected to greet total strangers with instant intimacy; must call them by their Christian names; enquire about husband, boyfriend, children. If she gets it wrong she has made a potential enemy for her employer. There is a famous Italian designer who, at one point in his career, invariably received lukewarm or bad press in Britain. At that time he was employing as head of his *service de presse* a woman generally considered if not the rudest, then certainly the coldest in Milan, so her employer failed to get the praise he often deserved.

Most designers only really trust those very close to them. In the 1980s the business partner came into his own as never before, paraded in the spotlight as adviser, inspiration and friend. Many were the lovers – or ex-lovers – of the designer. Some were their brothers and sisters. In Italy, in particular, they tended to be members of the family. In America, they were school or college buddies. Paul Poiret relied upon his wife to be the final arbiter; Chanel discussed her collections with Cocteau; Dior turned to Christian Bérard for advice and Schiaparelli involved Dali in many of her enterprises. But it is the in-house partnerships that matter. Balenciaga's right hand was his intimate friend and co-founder of the house, Vladzio d'Attainville, whose early death was a devastating blow which pushed Balenciaga into an inward-looking world of his own. Would Christian Dior have maintained his success so well without the support of his administrative director, Jacques Rouët, and his twin guardian angels, the legendary Germaine Bricard and Raymonde

Zehnacker? Would Jacques Fath have made it without his wife Geneviève at his side?

The tradition continues today. Gianni Versace – truly a man for keeping it in the family – employs his brother Santo as financial director and his brother-in-law, American ex-male model Paul Beck, to look after the menswear and work with his wife Donatella, Versace's sister, on the image projected by the Versace catalogue. But it is Donatella who is the true support for Versace, and her creative input is considerable. Critics have even suggested that Donatella has been the direct inspiration for many of Versace's more outrageous looks.

Another very intimate collaboration is the 34-year one between Valentino and his bellicose business partner Giancarlo Giammetti, who admits that their chance meeting in via Veneto in 1960 changed his life. Always immaculately tailored, impeccable of hair and faultlessly tanned, they seem almost too perfect a pair. Val and his friend love to party. They are seen at every social bash from Gstaad to LA, and are beloved of the ladies who lunch, who have a fetish about being seen with men who are supernaturally clean and have learned the secret of keeping age at bay. The designer admits freely that without his partner he could never have achieved so much.

When that kind of support is suddenly removed by death, as it was with Balenciaga, a crisis can develop. Giorgio Armani founded his firm with a friend, Sergio Galleotti, who became his managing director and, like Giammetti, his right hand. When Galleotti died in the mid-1980s, the event sparked worldwide speculation about the future of the firm he had helped Armani to build up. Could Armani cope alone? There were rumours that the firm might close. Armani nursed his grief silently and with dignity, plunging himself into work as Balenciaga had, determined to grow bigger and stronger just as he and his partner had planned. Those close to Armani at the time say that he set out to make Armani SpA a fitting memorial to his friend. Certainly he has done so by developing their joint dream, Armani Emporio – but not without help. His new right hand is his sister Rosanna who, tough, resourceful and energetic, has taken the place of Galleotti very successfully, at least in business terms.

The word 'polymath' is often used to describe Karl Lagerfeld. He designs under his own label and also for Chanel, for Chloé, and for Fendi of Rome. Few designers are so confident, or so openly contemptuous of the possibility of failure. And yet even Lagerfeld needs a sounding-board. He finds it in the designers he has appointed to develop and expand his ideas – Gilles Dufour at Chanel and Eric Wright at Chloé. One of Lagerfeld's great inspirations and business colleagues was Jacques de Bascher, whose place is now taken to a certain extent by Lagerfeld's friend and muse, Princess Diane de Beauvou-Gaon, whom he finds 'deeply spiritual'.

Unique in the fashion world is Milan's Bepe Modenese, who is friend, adviser and critic to many Italian designers. He runs Milan fashion week. Over six feet tall, Modenese is a man of genuine stature. His coolly diplomatic tongue is guaranteed to defuse the many explosive situations that are a part of daily life in Milan fashion circles. But he does more. He watches over the collections of several designers and corrects and guides their talents. I have seen him put together a show with an unerring eye, weeding out the dross from the gold with an objectivity which those more closely involved in the creative process often find difficult.

One of fashion's myths that persists despite all the clear evidence to the contrary is that designers are charming, even gentle, creatures who trip tentatively through the fashion jungle like tremulous Bambis. In reality many can be screaming harridans determined to have their way and ready to turn very nasty until they do. But this is conveniently hidden from the public by the fierce figure of the right-hand man or woman.

We are talking of people who can make strong men shrink and reduce beady-eyed journalists to tears. Patti Cohen at Donna Karan; Buffy Birrittelli at Ralph Lauren; Rita Airaghi at Ferre, all see a good part of their role as protection of the designer from hassle. The designer must smile, be relaxed, come over in public as reasonable, understanding and pleasant. Above all, as sane and everyday as you are.

10

The Titans

Calvin Klein, Ralph Lauren, Donna Karan: these three American designers, together with Giorgio Armani of Italy and the German Karl Lagerfeld, are the names with currency in design circles. Close behind come cult figures such as Jean Paul Gaultier, Dolce & Gabbana, and Romeo Gigli. Gianni Versace is a front runner. So is Yves Saint Laurent. Then there are all the ones who have had their moment – and may well have it again. People like Christian Lacroix and Azzedine Alaïa. There is also the 'lunatic' fringe, with people like Vivienne Westwood, Franco Moschino and John Galliano, whose names have resonance on the international gossip circuit, make circles, mean something to people only half interested in fashion. Even the Geordie TV detective, Spender, talks sneeringly of a rich woman in her Comme des Garçons and it can be assumed that producers feel that watchers of this prime-time series will understand the reference: designer name-dropping has gone global in the 1990s.

But it is Karan, Klein, Lauren, Armani and Lagerfeld – the Famous Five of fashion – who ultimately are the ones who *rate*. It is interesting to note the similarities between them. Only Lagerfeld stands slightly apart and different. An eclectic picker and plucker at the skirts of fashion history, taking and transforming things that have gone before, always heightening and dramatising them – fashion's equivalent of Walt Disney on acid – he is the only one of the five who still works to the traditional standards of French couture.

However, he is like the others in that he understands perfectly well that being a designer no longer simply means creating clothes. That particular skill is the basis of success, but it is not enough. These five have reached the top because they are skilled dressmakers, but they are also businessmen who have identified their market and developed advertising, marketing and retail strategies that put them in touch with it; and they are self-publicists, perfectly aware that the better their names are known, the more clothes they will sell.

Return to Camelot

Calvin Klein has said, 'I am a designer, not a star.' He knows it is not entirely true. Not that he would be very happy if it were. Stardom sells, as Klein, above all, should know. Was it not his star rating that made the Hollywood Bowl fashion show, which he compered for AIDS Project Los Angeles in 1992, such a sell-out that it pulled in $1 million for the charity – three times more than any previous APLA fund-raising event?

It was history's biggest fashion show, with 350 models and – proof of superstar designer status and its pulling power – *everybody* was there. The picnic dinner tables were so tightly packed that, according to *WWD*'s Eye report, 'Almost everyone managed to knock something over onto someone more powerful.' Especially when they all looked up to the plane overhead pulling a banner bearing the picture of rap star Marky Mark in Calvin underpants. It was very appropriate. Marky Mark is both the symbol and the reason why, after yet another difficult time, Calvin Klein is back up there in the superstar stratosphere.

That is where he has spent most of his working life, since he was first discovered by the New York store Bonwit Teller in 1968. Klein is a controversial figure. Many feel that he is the true father of the modern American fashion miracle, with talent and influence far greater than his arch-rival, Ralph Lauren. Others feel that he would be nowhere without Brooke Shields's bum and Marky Mark's crotch.

But what really signalled Calvin Klein's arrival as a world-class figure was the use of his name in Steven Spielberg's 1985 film *Back to the Future* in which Marty, played by Michael J. Fox, is whizzed back thirty years in time and meets his mother, Lorraine, when she is a teenager. Finding him unconscious after an accident and, unaware of his true identity, putting him to bed, she calls him Calvin. 'That is your name, isn't it?' she asks, 'It's written all over your underwear.' The important thing about featuring Calvin Klein underwear in such a blockbuster movie was that it was considered to have sufficient recognition to mean something not just to an American, but to a world, audience. It certainly did after the film was released.

Is it underwear that makes Klein's name synonymous with sexiness in fashion, or is it other aspects of his business – or even his own life – that do so? Klein is a gossip columnist's delight. But just what his name has symbolised in fashion terms for most people is hard to assess.

Obsession and Eternity are two of the best-known names in perfumery. Obsession is about *sexual* obsession in its many manifestations, including bisexuality, as the advertisements made clear. They are brilliantly provocative because they force people to recognise that their own sexuality is not always as straightforward as they would wish. The power of the ads can be judged by the fact that some were considered so shocking that they were banned – predictably enough, in Britain. Eternity took a softer, more romantic line, suggesting that love and family have lasting value.

Brooke Shields – once Valentino's muse and favourite model – made Klein's jeans famous in a highly competitive area of the market through the late Seventies ads where, pouting provocatively, she told us that nothing came between her and her Calvins and that, if they could talk, she would be 'ruined'. Sexuality in advertising had become overt, and these ads were slammed as 'lascivious'. TV networks took fright and banned some of them. Marvellous. Klein could not have orchestrated things better. Everyone was talking about him – and his jeans. Just as they did when he introduced a range of women's underwear modelled on men's Y-fronts. The fashion world, no stranger to perversity or the thrills of cross-dressing, shrieked with delight and took Calvin to its heart once again.

But that was the Eighties; this is now. Klein and his advertisers have always been able to judge to a nicety what will catch the world on the cusp between outrage and acceptability, and then give it to us just before we are ready, at the point when it still surprises but does not shock. Realising that the Nineties are at least as interested in the muscular young male body as in the female – and maybe more – Klein decided to put men's underwear back where it started. On men. Following a suggestion from the entertainment tycoon David Geffen, who in 1992 had acquired all outstanding debt securities of Calvin Klein Inc. (paying a reputed $31–41 million for bonds with a book value of $61–62 million), Klein decided to base his campaign on rap star Marky Mark and new waif superstar model Kate Moss.

Geffen, who had known Klein for many years, said when the business deal was completed, 'Calvin wins, I win,' adding, 'Listen, honey, it doesn't represent 5 per cent of my net worth.' Both sides of the agreement were emphatic that Geffen would interfere in no part of the business. But, of course, he could make suggestions, and it is generally accepted that he first floated the idea of the new ads featuring Marky Mark – firmly placing the emphasis on him rather than Moss. The ads, designed by fashion photographer Herb Ritts, appeared in print and made their TV début on MTV's *Rock 'N' Jock Basketball* slot. It was instant uproar time once more, with all the objections that had been thrown at the Brooke Shields and Obsession ads dusted off and used all over again. Disgusting, offensive, suggestive, sexist – at one point Marky Mark hugs the bare-breasted Kate Moss – the knee-jerk reaction must have been music to Klein and Geffen, as sales began to climb.

Nevertheless, Klein – again, possibly influenced by his friend – cut his advertising expenses for the third quarter of 1992 from almost $6 million to less than $2.5 million. A drop of this size is significant, but what is more interesting is the overall level of expense apparently required to keep a designer's name prominent. It is a sum that would make most British designers weep. They do not turn over that amount in a year's business, let alone one quarter – which is exactly why they have such a low profile. In fashion, as you pay, so are you known.

The Klein story continues to unfold. In the firm's first year wholesale revenues were $500,000, and Klein claimed that they rose by $1 million per year throughout the 1970s. By 1981 his annual income was estimated by *Fortune* magazine to be in the region of $8.5 million. In June 1993, when Klein borrowed $50 million from Citibank in order to buy back his bonds from Geffen, he was reputed to have an empire worth some $400 million at wholesale, with fragrances bringing in about $19 million. By any standards, these figures represent great success. But how much of it is based on Klein's success as a *designer*, and how much reflects his media profile?

As I have said, international success comes to designers not just because they design clothes that are right for their time but for a variety of interconnected reasons, not the least being how much capital can be made out of their personalities and way of life. Although in these days of endless celebrity interviews and appearances on TV, the designer must be hyped – and can be, by clever PR promotion, be he ne'er so dull – it is the way of life that is perhaps more important. There is something in human nature that needs to envy, that wishes to be made jealous, that longs to be outraged. When Sir James Goldsmith throws a party for his daughter in Paris, a surprisingly high number of people wish to read about it – marvelling at the mountains of beluga and the jazz band flown in from New Orleans. Of course, many more people are excited than repulsed, and enjoy a few minutes of fantasising about the rich over their morning mug of coffee. So with designers. It is not that they are only as good as their last collection. Increasingly, they are only as good as their last copy. That is why the Famous Five are always appearing in newspapers and magazines. It is also why a great designer such as Yves Saint Laurent has such a low international profile with the media. Rarely seen and never interviewed, there is nothing to write about, except his state of health over which there has been so much speculation that there is now nothing new to say. Gossip columnists can wait only for his death. Several times they have spread rumours of the event, as they have with Klein.

Like his clothes, Klein has slickly marketed himself and his image to his target customer. Handsome, charming, socially adept, he is fashion's John F. Kennedy – perpetually youthful in aura though ageing in actuality; straightforward and honest, although with hints of deliciously perverse peccadilloes but, above all, wearing that halo of undisputed success which attracts customers like a beacon.

The only flaw in the picture of Klein as one of the world's top five designers is his clothes. Unlike Armani and Lauren, Klein has not pursued world sales. But he has plans to open stores in Europe and the Far East in the 1990s. Whereas Lauren opened his first store outside North America (in London) in 1981, Klein's first free-standing foreign store was not opened until 1992, in Barcelona. Whereas Lauren has pushed his personality to the world as an extension – or even correction – to the American dream, Klein has been content with colonising the States through TV interviews and personal appearances at major stores across the continent. In February 1992 a personal appearance at I Magnin, San Francisco, resulted in $250,000-worth of sales in one afternoon; in Neiman Marcus, Dallas, a four-hour personal appearance pulled in $300,000.

But, bereft of the touch of personality and marketing magic, Calvin Klein's clothes have not always excited buyers outside America. Too often, on the racks they look bland, even banal. His laid-back assurance as a design minimalist makes women ask, 'What am I paying for?' Women who understand fashion and, ignoring the price tag, actually try on Klein's deceptively understated jackets and pants, know immediately. Klein's clothes are instant classics, as Giorgio Armani's are. A woman wearing clothes bought from either designer's range fifteen years ago could walk into the smartest reception today and still look right. That is why Calvin Klein is much more than the sum of his spectacularly successful perfume ads.

But perhaps, like Jack Kennedy, Klein's success rests on something more basic. National heroes are made of those who seem to reflect all that is best in a nation's characteristics. Klein's power lies in the fact that he, his clothes and his attitude to publicity are all bedrock USA. Like Bruce Springsteen, he was made there, made it there and, as a result, could find the world at his feet as we move towards the new century.

Fashion's Archivist

If it is true that Calvin Klein still makes Ralph Lauren nervous, it is not so surprising. Like Klein, Lauren is a brilliant merchandiser and knows that, in part, his success depends on selling himself and the lifestyle in which he believes. He has been so successful at doing this that he is far and away America's richest and best-known designer.

If there is something louche about Klein, there is something slightly risible about Lauren – not as a designer, but as a man.

Although his clothes are beautiful, desirable and wearable, the source of his inspiration is perhaps suspect. He originally made his money by taking a deep American longing and fleshing it in clothes. He took his inspiration from the cowpoke West – a cleaned-up, sanitised, Glenn Ford version. Lauren was the mean streets city boy dreaming of the wide plains, long horizons and huge skies of Colorado, Montana and Texas. As an inspiration it was a cliché and maybe that was what made Lauren's vision so attractive to millions of urban, high-rise homesteaders. Lauren's Western clothing was made for weekend role-playing, and it is part of his genius for knowing what very ordinary people fantasise about in America – land of the *free*, after all – that enabled him to clothe their fantasies with the right stuff. The very banality of Lauren's Western vision struck an answering chord in millions of city-based country lovers.

It was a short and even logical step from that fantasy to a James Dean, Rock Hudson, 'Giant' dream of the *wealth* of the West – the thoroughbred yearlings; the mahogany-trimmed pick-up trucks; Gene Tierney and Lauren Bacall oozing class in perfectly simple – and simply perfect – silk shirts and jodhpurs; and then to what made it all possible – the black liquid under the plains. Lauren fell in love all over again, and this time the objects of his desire were the Western aristocrats in their highly polished, hand-made riding boots, immaculate London-tailored riding pants and custom-made stetsons. From them it was just another short step to yacht clubs on Rhode Island, family mansions by the sea, tennis parties, croquet on the lawn, cruising in the Caribbean, crossing to Europe and Paris, the South of France – the dream of freedom again, as seen through Hollywood eyes.

He chooses to sell his clothes in a converted New York mansion on the Upper East Side in which whatever was lacking in Edwardian splendour has been lovingly created. Shopping at the Rhinelander building is like no other shopping experience in the world, but it leaves one feeling queasy. What are these carefully contrived tableaux of old photographs, well-worn books and silver cigarette boxes saying? Why do we accept the concept of a fossilised private home being used to sell modern merchandise? What are we expected to feel as we climb that mahogany staircase and gaze up at the family portraits and conversation pieces that line the walls?

Lauren's great discovery, in an egalitarian society like North America, is that people are snobs.

Lauren has said, 'What I do is what I am', and his preposterous lifestyle shows how totally he has been sucked into his own fantasy. He is cowboy, aviator, white hunter, film director, land-owning squire – and he has the clothes, the props *and* the photographs to prove it.

'Ready when you are, Mr de Mille.' We are Lauren's cast of thousands and he is our director, complete with brilliantly polished riding boots and 1930s hacking jacket, herding us into his perfectly recreated period stage set where – look, but don't touch – we are urged forward by his loud-hailer to the ever-ready cash tills as we buy a replica, a facsimile of the real thing which, until Lauren appeared, had long been discarded. And we *love* it. This is the crowd scene we all want to play.

Perhaps it is because their history is comparatively short that Americans so value their past. Mystic Sea Port, Dearborn Village, Williamsburg – historical societies lavish time and money on accurate reconstructions of history, and the population rewards them by flocking to look. Ralph Lauren is fashion's historical society, the Rhinelander is his site – and we make the pilgrimage not merely to see, but to buy the results of his archaeological digs.

In my opinion, Lauren is the world's most romantic designer, creating clothes not merely beautiful and desirable in themselves but bringing with them an aura of a gracious and elegant past. But one must remember the origin of these clothes. The originals on which they were based were worn, in the main, by people living vain and worthless lives. The fact that at the end of the most egalitarian century in history Ralph Lauren has made us desire such clothes shows how completely he has uncovered the dross in us all. It is a sad reflection that, after a hundred years of free, compulsory education, the new rich (and the less rich) are so lacking in vision and self-esteem that they still wish to ape the old rich and their social attitudes. As Pierre Bergé has said, 'He represents all that I detest in fashion. He appeals to people who want to hide in the past.'

And there are a lot of them about. Lauren's commercial success has been phenomenal. In 1991 Polo Ralph Lauren clocked up $3.1 billion in retail volume. He now has 145 stores, most of which are in the US and the rest scattered across the globe from London to Japan and the Pacific Rim. The fact that he has shops in South Korea and Malaysia shows the extent of a vision so powerful that it cuts across cultural and ethnic barriers to bring everyone into one huge Hollywood fantasy, where the coolies and lascars of the real times Lauren takes us back to can forget their slave status and play at being the wide-eyed white Westerner, taking tea from a table covered with a Lauren cloth lovingly remade from the past.

The man who told the *Daily News*, way back in 1979, 'I can do anything I want, there's nothing I can't have' (and who, a year previously, had been described in *WWD* as wearing a 'got-it-made aura like a label'), is limited by only one thing – himself. His approach to the past, hailed as patrician, is reminiscent of that other great American tycoon, Jay Gatsby, whose every action exemplified the vulgarity of vast wealth when it is divorced from cultural anchors. Just as Gatsby had his taste created by proxy, employing 'little men' in London to select his shirts for him, so Lauren has his tastes made by a world he has not experienced. But whereas Gatsby went for the best that money can buy, Ralph Lauren's Rhinelander building – I almost wrote 'experience' –

betrays his Airfix kit approach to the past. All the stage props against which the merchandise is displayed reveal his cheap, ready-to-assemble cultural sympathies. In a mélange of English country house meets Whitehall farce, he homes in on the worthless, expendable items found below stairs and buys them up with the same crassness with which some people assemble libraries of fine bindings, buying by the yard, not the title. There is no Berenson working diligently through the great European houses for Lauren. Instead, teams of stylists hunt out the trivial, the second-rate, the unimportant artefacts against which to display a way of life to which we are expected to aspire.

Lauren's researchers squirrel up job lots from remote house sales and their finds are uncritically displayed. The Rhinelander staircase is covered with pictures which would not be given wall space in the upstairs back corridor of a remote Scottish manse. And yet, all of this tat is hailed as a merchandising miracle. There is something akin to walking on water in Lauren's achievement. He has, after all, been able to sell some of the world's most expensive clothing to many of the world's most sophisticated shoppers by these servants'-entrance tactics.

The fabric of the past – the image of the present: they sum up Ralph Lauren and Calvin Klein. Both from the Bronx, neither from the 'top drawer', they have, together, brilliantly mirrored the two sides of the society in which they live. It is popular to dismiss them both as nothing more than super-stylists or mega-merchandisers. European journalists and designers do so all the time. But it is a slur – and it completely misunderstands what modern fashion is about.

Female Friends

Modern women do not require clothes that need a special frame of mind or an assumed attitude. They want to be as relaxed in their dress as the average man. They also want to have allure and sex appeal. But on their own terms. Enter the third Manhattan fashion power, Donna Karan.

Like Lauren himself, Karan has made a leap that in European terms is almost inconceivable, if not impossible. She has gone from unknown, unnamed designer on Seventh Avenue, working for the Anne Klein label, to named designer (with Louis dell' Olio) for that label, then to designer in her own right with her own label, backed initially by the owners of the Anne Klein label itself. This is an exceptional track record and reflects the burning ambition of a woman who has gone from mass to class, and is actively working to bring class back to the mass – at a price.

Every successful designer has a special merchandising touch that finds an answering chord not previously played. Karan's unique ploy was to identify an uncatered-for market and exploit it for all it was worth. She started her own-name line in 1985, the moment when American feminism was beginning to wonder just how much the sisterhood could unbend, just how far they could go without becoming 'man-bait' again. The woman who dreamed up the advertising slogan 'In Women We Trust' knew precisely how to help them. Like a Girl Scout leader or a school trip organiser, Karan popped up waving a huge banner which screamed in mile-high letters 'Follow me!' And they did. Because they trusted. Here was a woman – a liberated, fulfilled and proven businesswoman – saying, 'Get out in the marketplace. Use your talents. Don't take any more shit from men.' They had heard it all before, of course. What made the Karan message so irresistible was the rider: 'And I will dress you for the part. Trust me; a woman, a feminist. I will give you clothes that fit your dignity as a woman, your role in a man's world, and still ensure that you are in charge.' Overnight, 'Dress for Success' – which encouraged women to become surrogates in men's clothes – was seen for the fatuous, sexist rubbish it was. *Real* women – Karan women – dressed not for success but because they already *were* a success, on every level.

They needed to be. Karan's 'five easy pieces' approach to the modern woman's wardrobe – all skilfully wrapped and draped cashmere – did not carry a bargain basement price tag.

Karan is the nearest American fashion gets to pure showbiz. Not in her clothes but her personal projection. As subtle as a killer shark, as restful as a South Sea hurricane, she is high-octane, running away at the mouth at the slightest opportunity, mega-decibelling everyone and everything with an overwhelming enthusiasm for everything Donna does, Donna thinks, Donna believes and Donna dreams. It is not surprising that Barbra Streisand, another understated personality, should be Donna's best buddy. They both live on noise. However, all the hype, all the shouting, all the cheap philosophising and 'sincerity' cannot disguise the two central facts about Karanism.

Firstly, the clothes, whether from her full-price or second, DKNY, labels, are prefectly attuned to the way modern women wish to dress. Secondly, the psychology. It is *because* Karan is so loudly, triumphantly, immoderately successful that women want to buy her clothes. Karan *convinces* them that these clothes will do for them what they have done for her: that is, put them on top in a man's world. That is why the cult of the clothes is so firmly based on the cult and character of their creator – just as with Lauren and Klein.

In February 1992, Donna Karan made a personal appearance at Bergdorf's in New York, doing, as *WWD* reported, 'what she does best – schmooze with her most loyal customers'. The day began with breakfast for eighty-five big spenders, followed by a fashion show. Then they hit the boutique on the third floor and went through the Karan merchandise like a horde of locusts. Result: Bergdorf's biggest ever trunk show, with a sales high of $400,000 by the end of the day. And this is why Karan, who began her firm with a start-up capital of $3 million, had a sales volume of $270 million in 1992 and was able to borrow $110 million from Citibank in 1993 to facilitate expansion plans. This is retail magic in the grand American manner and is based on a closely focused sales pitch. Donna Karan has created the myth that she is not just her customer writ large but, in fact, *all* women. Trading on her sex, she declares that she *really* knows her customer, the inference being that male designers are denied this intimacy. When Karan says, 'My body tells me what she wants . . . I travel, I work, I understand her chaos . . . I understand . . . I understand what it's like . . .' she is twisting women in an emotional armlock no less powerful because it is spurious. Donna believes it; so do they. And sales just rise and rise.

The American dream is based not on abstracts, not on hypotheses, not on supposition. It is essentially a *practical* dream rooted in the reality of the individual who has made it. Read any American magazine, from *Vanity Fair* to *Forbes*, and you will discover that money only becomes interesting when linked to a personality. Success only becomes understandable when it is clothed in human form. The same is true of fashion. American women do not just buy clothes: they spend their money in order to buy into a lifestyle – a lifestyle linked to a person who has made it and is *doing* it. That is why Karan commandeers more inch-space in *Women's Wear Daily* than any other designer; that is why a personal appearance in a store can push sales up to record levels; that is why she makes videos and look-books for stores so that customers can be in no doubt at all how Donna wishes them to appear this season. Although still far behind Klein and Lauren in sales, Donna Karan is moving up. The Nineties will be hers and she will need some very bad luck to stop her ensnaring the world's women.

Klein, Lauren and Karan have all diluted their original fashion message by taking on board movements from Europe. But as they have broadened their appeal they have weakened what many commentators see as their great strength, which is their very

Americanism. Public perception of the Holy Trinity is already lagging behind the current reality. Lauren's Western looks were a late-Seventies, early-Eighties statement. He has moved on through Rhode Island 'royalty' to Admiral's Cup fancy dress, with all shades of glamour taken in on the way. Klein's Hamptons/Fire Island looks – young, *dégagé* and arrogantly casual – have been modified over the last ten years to have an appeal very similar to the best Milanese fashion, and Karan has broadened her spectrum to include a much more overt sexuality than the sisterhood would have found acceptable at the outset of her career.

All have succumbed to the creeping internationalism which is one of the major strands of fashion in the 1990s, but only canny old Ralph has seen the danger signs. That is why he has gone back to his roots. As long ago as 1978, Lauren nailed his colours to the mast with his proclamation that 'Western is as real as Harris tweed – classic, ageless and yet youthful.' In autumn 1993, he opened his Polo Sporting Club store at 888 Madison Avenue, opposite his 72nd Street flagship Polo Ralph Lauren store, to sell his dream all over again. Double RL (which stands for Ricky and Ralph Lauren), his newest range, is the core of the store. It is Western with a capital W. As *WWD* described it, Double RL is for 'any dude who wants to look like he's spent a hard day rustling cattle'. In other words, the Lauren vision for the late Nineties is about urban cowboys, the most ersatz of all the suspect semiotic groups spawned in the last twenty years. What is worrying about this sterile, *déjà vu* approach to dress is the feeling one gets that Lauren is almost certainly correct to describe Double RL as being, 'About America, whether you're 50 or 18, whether you're a man or a woman. It's timeless. I wore it when I was 18 and I wear it now.' And a million hopefuls storm the doors of Polo Sporting Club every week, searching for something, anything, from the past that will make the future go away. Thanks for the memory, Ralph – you just might be forging the new internationalism for the twenty-first century.

Cool-hand Luke

The leader of the current internationalist pack is a strange, humourless and obsessive man who rarely leaves his palazzo in Milan, only travels beyond Italy reluctantly and apparently lacks interest in anything apart from clothes. Giorgio Armani *is* internationalism in Nineties fashion, as he has been for a dozen years now. It couldn't have happened to a less likely person. Armani is austere, he is remote, he is non-communicative and yet he has the pulse of women. He knows what they want. The reason, he maintains, is that his clothes are based on one thing – the logic of the times. The modern logic of design is functional, to do with suitability of purpose, understanding of material and rejection of gratuitous decorative additions. Wearability is the only criterion, according to the Armani philosophy.

Sound familiar? You bet. It was Chanel who said that clothes must be logical and it is from *her* philosophy that Armani has come. Like Abstract Expressionists, they both believe that the couturier's intervention should be minimal, allowing the material to make its own gesture. In painting terms, this leads to random results and this is where Armani and his mentor are different not only from the Abstract Expressionists, but also from most designers of the last fifty years. There is nothing random about an Armani jacket, any more than there was in a Chanel suit. It is the result of a rigorous examination of the nature of a jacket, the nature of the female body and the nature of the life in which it is to be worn. Armani does not start work on a design with a preconceived decorative element in mind. Like an engineer or architect, he sees design in terms of problem-solving. The more rational the solution, the more successful the design.

It is an approach that has produced the only clothing in the last forty years of the twentieth century that has the undisputed right to be called 'classic'. The Armani jacket (like the pants and soft blouse, and gathered skirt!) evolved in the early 1980s, defined a decade and has been worn by women of all sizes and shapes worldwide. It was copied, reproduced and adapted by the fashion world at every level of manufacture from the highest to the lowest. And its influence will continue for decades to come because its logic is so impeccable that it cannot legitimately be superseded. But it will continue for another, even more basic reason. It not only flatters a woman, it comforts her by disguising her faults; it encourages her by taking fashion gaucherie and transforming it into assurance; and it never makes her feel she is wearing fancy dress. For these reasons, the Armani-clad woman is inviolable. Unlike those dressed by other designers, she *never* looks ridiculous; she *always* maintains her dignity. That is why Giorgio Armani is the fashion leader of the world.

But there is more to the Armani miracle. This silver-haired, bespectacled recluse, a man who will soon be 60, who gives interviews only when he has to, appears in public only when he must and attends parties only if essential, has understood and defined youth dressing for both sexes for the last ten years. Like every other successful designer, Armani is marketing himself. The Armani spirit is about the dream of eternal youth which takes his normally cool and formal personality and makes it, if not playful, then certainly laid back. Emporio, Armani A/X Exchange, Armani Jeans are all labels dedicated to casual, confident youth. For that reason alone his shops are full of people of all ages. The sales figures show the phenomenal success of the concept. In 1992, sales of the top-price, Black Label Borgonuovo line, which Armani has described as showing his creativity to the limit, reached $72 million; Emporio made $78 million which, when added to jeans sales, gave a total of $167 million.

Ever since its inception in 1985, Emporio has hit the spot with people who want to be laid back and elegant at the same time. Its extraordinary success is reflected in the fact that, by the end of

1995, there will be 120 stores worldwide. They will present the shopper with an experience that goes far beyond the mere purchase of a sweatshirt or pair of jeans. Like Lauren, Armani understood early on the necessity of ambience, if casual clothing was to acquire the mystique necessary to persuade people to pay the sort of prices that no one had previously had the balls to suggest for simple denim shirts and white T-shirts. His vision of shopping was bogus, but not nearly as ham as Lauren's merchandising into a history that never was. Armani created The Shop as Ship – all bleached floorboards, chrome and glass in the Twenties tradition. Like Polo Ralph Lauren, Armani, including Emporio, was a shopping experience of privilege. It was an honour to buy in such surroundings. And Armani's taupe carrier bag with its refined black writing was an even greater status symbol than Polo's navy and gold. Of *course* the prices were justified! To get that sort of lift costs a thousand bucks at any halfway-decent shrink!

A Brief History of Time

In many ways, the bag was as talismanic as the purchase. Shopping bags have become much more than the potential detritus of a played-out culture: they have become the symbol of that culture. And people aspire to both culture and packaging. That is why today Chanel, the name, has a power greater than in the days of Coco herself. But a shopping bag is still just a shopping bag, even with those bewitching Cs in sharp black and white. It is what the initials stand for that matters. Chanel shopping bags are not desirable for the irascible spirit of the old guardian of rue Cambon but for that of the present incumbent. Karl Lagerfeld is the only international designer who genuinely gives the impression that he does not care about the approbation of press or public. He can afford to be cavalier. After all, he is only the hired hand – even his own-name firm is owned by Dunhill. And if all the people he works for sacked him tomorrow, one suspects that it would mean very little to the multi-millionaire Lagerfeld, who once claimed he wore his pigtail so that he would not be mistaken for a banker.

But Lagerfeld is so instinctive a designer that making him stop would be like forbidding him to breathe. Although he has been designing for as long as Yves Saint Laurent and Valentino, he has not suffered their fate. YSL still creates the most beautiful clothes in Paris, but his inspiration has become rather dusty. Valentino works to an ideal of womankind that has not been current for thirty years. Neither couturier is considered a pace-setter. Lagerfeld has avoided the problem of middle-aged men by renewing himself constantly.

How does he do it? his fellow designers ask in despair. I believe his secret lies in a kind of greed. Karl Lagerfeld must have *all* the experiences the world has to offer. He does not buy one CD at a time, he buys 300. He has not just amassed a library of fashion books, he has created *the* fashion library, which contains virtually every book written on the subject for the last 200 years. He does not content himself with one beautiful home (but then, what success-ful designer does?) – he must have four, furnished in styles that sweep from Versailles to Memphis.

It is Lagerfeld's very eclecticism that makes him unsatisfactory. He has too many restless talents and he finds it too easy to exploit them. He seems incapable of staying still long enough to build on what he has achieved. As long ago as 1977 American fashion journalist Nina Hyde saw Lagerfeld as 'the rare designer who starts every season from scratch'. She meant to praise, but surely this is exactly what is at the root of Lagerfeld's problem. He has a terror of being old-fashioned. He is petrified of getting into a rut. So he spins around like a Catherine wheel, sparking ideas, many of which are brilliant but which he will never fully develop.

Lagerfeld covers his trail with drop-dead aphorisms carefully crafted to tell little but to look good on the page. He skims across the surface of fashion, determined not to touch down, determined to treat it all as ephemeral, determined not to be judged. 'Nothing is serious in life,' he declares, trying to convince us that he is a social butterfly indifferent to and unaware of the world's problems. 'I don't compete, I don't compare,' he cries, baffling any attempt to 'place' him in the international fashion team. 'Designers don't really make any great contribution,' he suggests, implying that even if his fellows are pompously full of self-importance, he is not. 'I respect nothing, no one, including myself. Respect is not a very creative thing. . . . It is not amusing not to change, it is the beginning of retirement. . . . The more people are talking about me, the more good I'm doing for everybody.' The torrent of words spills out, the smokescreen grows thicker, hiding this apparently most open but actually most secret of men. But, out of all the 'candid' quotes, perhaps the most revealing of Lagerfeld the creator is his remark that he is a fashion nymphomaniac who never has an orgasm.

But if he fails as a great designer, Lagerfeld succeeds as an influence. He really is an extraordinarily witty and inventive designer. Like a juggler, he can keep more balls in the air than anyone else – and they are the brightest, most colourful balls in the circus. Lagerfeld knows this, as he knows his skills. So does the whole fashion world. Sections of it feed and get fat each season on the ideas Lagerfeld tosses off with scarcely a pause. He does not wait, he does not reflect. He lets others do that. He is entirely spontaneous. He constantly breaks new ground.

When twenty-first-century historians assess Lagerfeld's place in fashion, they will see that he presided over a singular and important change of emphasis in the way we look at clothes. He is the designer who has smashed through the prison wall of good taste that was last repointed in the 1950s and has remained intact ever since. Unlike a marauding Goth of fashion, he has done so from the inside, from the fashion Holy of Holies, the *haute couture*.

Unlike Versace, who broke the rules of taste because he knew no better, or Lacroix, who broke them in a 'Look what *I've* done' spirit of nursery naughtiness, Lagerfeld broke them in perfect knowledge of what he was doing, because they were old-fashioned and inappropriate.

In spite of his eclectic, rag-bag borrowing from every fashion period in the last 200 years, Lagerfeld is the most modern designer working in Paris. He has not only redefined taste; he has demolished it by his constant questioning of fashion's received wisdom. 'Who cares?' is one of his favourite ripostes. And the answer is that nobody does now, thanks to him. Taste, the exclusive preserve of the informed mind, has gone, in fashion as in everything else. And with it, the rules have been swept aside. Fashion is at last able to breathe, to expand, to move forward. This is Lagerfeld's lasting achievement. He has redrawn the map as convincingly as Joseph Beuys, Schoenberg and even James Joyce have in their fields of endeavour. It is a map for the twenty-first century that makes the one that most of Paris is still following seem as old-fashioned and uninformed as one showing the earth to be flat: 'Here be monsters.'

11

Masks and Faces

Would fashion exist if mirrors had not been invented? Do we dress in order to derive pleasure and confidence from our mirror image? To be admired by others? or to emulate our peers or social superiors? Traditionally commentators have come down heavily in favour of the idea that a woman dresses to attract or keep a man. The concept, like most of our lingering attitudes to the sexes, is largely a Victorian one. Modern women know it is nonsense. It is not especially surprising, however, that at the end of the twentieth century men cling to attitudes evolved in the nineteenth. Victorian sophistry loaded the dice in favour of their sex. The decorative woman, dressed to reflect well on the male, is a comforting concept for the majority of men, even today.

In the nineteenth century, as in earlier centuries, society was organised almost entirely around the needs of men – especially those in the upper and middle classes. Men saw divorce as personally embarrassing and socially destabilising. Hence women were taught, as they had been for generations, to honour and obey. So inferior was the status of the female sex that the inclusion of a clause in the marriage ceremony stating that men must, at least, consult women on matters of joint involvement was never contemplated. Today, the promise to obey is not part of the marriage proceedings – but then, neither is the need to consult.

In 1808 *La Belle Assemblée*, a magazine aimed at upper- and middle-class urban women, was advising them to 'read frequently with close attention the matrimonial service, and take care in doing it not to overlook the word OBEY'. Such was the indoctrination of the age that the editor could be sure that the sentiment would be greeted with nods of approval by female readers – and even more vigorous ones from any male who might have picked up the magazine in an idle moment.

Before the passing of the first English divorce law in 1857, a wife's body was seen as part of a husband's property rights. When Fielding's Mr Modern in *The Modern Husband*, published in 1732, tells his wife 'Your Person is mine; I bought it lawfully in church,' he was not merely being cynical, he was stating a fact in law. A husband who felt this presumably would also expect to have some say in how that body should be clothed. Not that the average man cared about female fashion. What he cared about, much as husbands do now, was that his wife should not embarrass him, either socially or financially, by her dress.

Essentially clothes are a part of social etiquette. They must conform to the standards accepted within a class and social hierarchy. In the past, fashionable female dress was not worn merely to make a woman look physically and sexually attractive. The semiotics of fashionable clothing were much more complex. They reflected the status, breeding, wealth and power, not only of the woman but also of the man to whom she was married, the family of which she was a part and the class in which she lived. And the class which wore fashionable clothes up to a brief forty years ago was almost exclusively the upper class. Only upper-class women had the leisure and wealth to indulge a passion for fashion. Of all women, they alone were able to accept the constraints and inconvenience of fashionable dress because they alone had no activity to perform which awkward status clothing would have made impossible. The sheer impracticality of fashionable dress was one of its greatest attractions. Towering head-dresses from the medieval hennin to the Edwardian picture hat laden with roses, feathers, even whole birds; long trains, wide loops and trailing hemlines; bustles and hobbled ankles all made for immobility. They turned fashionable women into creatures with no other purpose than to be looked at; creatures incapable of moving with anything like alacrity, let alone working with physical vigour. They were a clear indication of a class power – even a right – to be indolent, and to be served by others, just as the distant gatehouse and long drive were physical barriers to keep all but personal servants and guests at bay.

Even as late as the 1950s, fashionable dress was neither comfortable nor convenient. The New Look relied on the underpinning of wired bras, heavily boned corsets and padded hips for its full effect. A couture dress, interlined, with skirts often padded, weighted shoulders stuffed with horse hair, and lines at such variance with those of the female body that they constrained movement, was a status garment. It told the world that its wearer, if not rich herself, was married to a rich man. If not married, then kept. Women who earned their own living rarely paid huge prices for couture. Why should they spend a fortune on clothing so uncomfortable and impractical? It must be remembered that couture customers allowed dress to play a major role in their lives and gave time to it that women with an occupation could not afford. Quite apart from hours spent in fittings, at the *corsetière*, choosing accessories, with the hairdresser and manicurist, it was not unusual for a fashionable lady in the 1950s to change her clothing up to three times a day during the town season. By the time the 1960s were half over, the philosophy behind this form of status dressing was discredited. Women – especially young women – wished to be independent of men and chose their clothing to reflect their attitude and the amount of time they were prepared to devote to dress.

The pages of fashion magazines in the Seventies reflect another change. The new status in dress was to do with imponderables such as taste, style, personality and wit. Above all, it was to do with

193

individuality. But, even in the vanguard days of women's libera-
tion, women still needed the extravagant and impractical. Old
indoctrinations die hard. They found what they needed in couture
but, even more, in the models who showed it. The model Verushka
became a star because she was impractical – too tall, too beautiful
to be real. Women who felt guilt at the excitement of viewing
glamorous 'kept-woman' couture shifted the guilt, but managed to
retain their New Woman credentials and continued to enjoy the
things their sisters dubbed reprehensible by blaming the model.
She was the traitor, the woman who writhed before the cameras of
the male photographer, like Verushka in Antonioni's cult film,
Blow-Up.

No fashion exists in a vacuum. There must always be a mirror.
Women still need to look at impractical idealisations of femininity,
just as they did when grand, overdressed ladies descended from
their coaches into the seething streets. It is not only women who
need this fantasy. We all do. And it is provided for us in the pages of
fashion magazines.

Vogue was conceived by Condé Nast to be a primer for the very
rich of both sexes. In World War I it was the favourite magazine of
trench-bound officers. Today, it is read by hairdressers, shop
assistants, make-up artists, stylists, photographers, layout artists,
boutique owners, art editors, manufacturers, designers and everyone involved in fashion, no matter how peripherally, of either sex,
not one of whom might wish to buy the clothes featured in its
pages. To those readers, *Vogue* is as the *Burlington Magazine* is to
art experts or *Sight and Sound* to the film industry – an organ of
information.

Vogue, like all high fashion magazines, assumes that every day
begins with a new fashion dawn – abstract, pure and fresh.
Women's magazines are different. They do not note the dawn; it is
the common light of day that interests them. The dedicated
follower of fashion barely gives them a glance, even though

women buy them in much greater numbers than the glossies. But, for all the guilt that the modern woman might feel about 'rich-bitch' dressing or 'kept-woman' clothes, the excitement of exotic dress cannot be stilled. The guilt must be shifted. Fashion models personify the dreams of thousands of women who wish to dress in status clothes but dare not. That is why the pages of fashion magazines give such vicarious pleasure and are such a telling mirror for the fantasies of the age.

Sixty years ago Chanel told her models, 'Confidence is contagious and I want my customers to catch it from you.' Easing customers into spending serious amounts of money requires a psychological approach, and it is in acknowledgement of the role they play in this psychological war game that models are so handsomely rewarded. The fact that so few women do buy what the models peddle – high fashion clothes are still the exception in most Western countries and almost totally the exception in the East – can be seen either as a failure of the model or a triumph of common sense. But it is probably true that for every woman who wishes to identify with Kate Moss, there are at least ten who would prefer to be like Anna Nicole or Eva Herzigova, the voluptuous models for Guess jeans.

There are even more who would like an older role model, as cosmetic firms have realised. Yves Saint Laurent's *femme mûre* to promote his beauty line is Catherine Deneuve, who is 50. Anouk Aimée, who promotes Ungaro perfumes, is the same age. Isabella Rossellini, employed to promote the image of Lancôme, is 40. All three are the sort of woman other women would like to be. All three are beauties, but their beauty is less than perfect, blurred by character and experience. They can be believed in to an extent that younger models cannot. Claudia Schiffer may well have 10,000 expressions, as is claimed by fashion's quality controller, Karl Lagerfeld, but how many women can identify with her when each expression appears the same as the last? Does a contract with

Revlon for $10 million redeem her in the eyes of her public from the paranoia of insisting on a special changing cubicle at Chanel for fear of peeping Toms?

Schifferism abounds in fashion, even with those drafted in for only a short spell at the coalface. Isabelle Adjani, the French film star, was hired as its personality by the house of Dior when they relaunched Miss Dior in October 1992 in a campaign reputed to cost over FF 1 million. Miss Adjani walked down the runway at the Dior show, wearing an unbelievable concoction and clutching the hand of its perpetrator, Gianfranco Ferre. That evening she was star guest at the party in honour of the scent, a role for which she was suitably rewarded. Suddenly, Schifferism struck and Miss Adjani insisted that only photographers who had signed a contract might take her picture. Those who had not and were impertinent enough to have them published would be fined FF 100,000!

When Versace says, 'Supermodels are the stars of my show', nobody would argue, although many might question his judgement when he adds, 'I respect them highly.' Of course, Christy Turlington's ability rests on more than her bee-sting lips; Tatjana Patitz has more than sleeping-sickness eyes; Linda Evangelista's hooked nose-end is not her only attribute any more than are Cindy Crawford's beauty spot or Naomi Campbell's sofa lips. They all have much more than their looks to make them stand out on the catwalk. They have command – the ability to order and control their space and make audiences and photographers take notice. Every show and photographic session presents a challenge: to bring out the style, subtlety and character of the designer's intentions. That is why top models enjoy working for top designers and photographers. It is not just that it gives them a high profile. It is much more the challenge of something to live up to, in the creations of a maestro.

The result of Linda Evangelista's fashion shoot for Marks and Spencer were eerily unfocused. A million-dollar glamour presence in high street clothing seemed as bizarre a juxtaposition as a Ferrari towing a caravan. We do not want to see supermodels looking normal.

Designers no longer create with a vaguely idealised woman in mind. They take as their muse a model type – and the fashion direction of the 1990s will not evolve until the battle of the models is resolved. On one side are the supermodels: proven money-spinners who launched a thousand products in the 1980s. They are still the darlings of the advertisers, despite the gibes that their super-elegance is little more than drag-queen culture. They are the dream-peddlers of fashion imagery. On the other side stand the gamines and super-waifs led by Kate Moss and Claudia Mason; and a one-woman band called Kristen McMenary. It will be interesting to see how long McMenary survives; fashion soon becomes bored with unconventionality.

Naomi topples – and the world sits up. At a time when hard news was at its hardest, with atrocities in Bosnia, famine in Somalia and the world's finances close to collapse, Naomi Campbell effortlessly scooped the front pages when she slipped and fell while showing Vivienne Westwood's collection for autumn 1993.

For those who feel that fashion has undergone a radical change in the 1990s, Naomi's fall confirmed the long-anticipated collapse of the supermodel circus which has dominated fashion's big tops throughout the world for more than ten years. Routed by the new waiflike models, Linda Evangelista, Claudia Schiffer, Carla Bruni *et al.* were, according to the popular press, finished, surplus to cultural requirements and ready to be put out to grass. And yet they were such damned good copy that the very fashion writers eager to write them off could not, when the time came, bear to part with them, any more than designers or photographers could, even though they wanted to pay them much less than in the Eighties.

And, no matter how much designers like Calvin Klein or photographers like Steven Meisel might love Kate Moss for the very fact that her ordinariness was not writ large, we the public needed more. Even if all models are basically the girl next door, we do not want them to be *too* girl next door. We still long for Naomi on the arm of Robert de Niro or some other suitably high-profile escort; we still hanker after the in-your-face vulgarity of Linda who joked that she would not get out of bed for less than $10,000 a day. Beauty is not enough; we need something unattainable. Super-models give us glamour by proxy without the need personally to experience the rigours of dieting, the tedium of sitting around in photographers' studios for hours as make-up artists paint and hairdressers frizz our personalities away, or the sheer slog of doing eight shows a day in Paris, Milan or New York.

They are the mercenaries of the fashion world whose huge earning potential and high profile are exciting for us all. They are paid handsomely for the use of their bodies – Helena Christensen has been known to earn £40,000 a week during the collections, Linda Evangelista and Cindy Crawford were each paid £77,000 for a Kookaï campaign. Their job is to conquer. It is also to quell. Supermodels are not used merely to show clothes, but to show them in a way that overwhelms criticism.

In the Fifties we had model girls, a name suggestive of im-maturity, even stupidity. And the name epitomised the product. Models in the Fifties made no demands, were not part of fashion power politics and were treated with indifference if not contempt by the people whose clothes they were paid to show. They were, in the terminology of the day, clothes-horses. Diana Vreeland once told me that Balenciaga talked of his customers as horses whose role was not to think but to be guided in every particular of dress by the maestro as super-jockey. His attitude – extreme in relation to customers – was standard as far as model girls were concerned. Richard Avedon, doyen of Fifties fashion photographers, con-demned them as underdeveloped, frightened and insecure women, most of whom, in his opinion, had been considered ugly when children because they were long and thin. But, like straggling plants reaching up to the light, they blossomed in a way that made Avedon's remarks churlish, considering how these underdeveloped, frightened and insecure women helped make his name and fortune. If it was all a charade, it was a brilliantly convincing one. Suzy Parker, China Machado, Margot McKendry, Barbara Goalen, Fiona Campbell-Walter, Jean Dawnay: all managed to look the epitome of sophisticated, worldly womanhood on the outside, regardless of how they might feel on the inside.

The 1950s was the last period when hauteur was not only part of the currency of fashion but its *raison d'être*. In the 1960s it was supplanted by youthful liveliness, which gave place in the 1970s to a dreamy wistfulness. At the end of the decade this was changed dramatically and permanently by the introduction of black models on the runway. But in the 1950s a model would get nowhere if she did not come over as a lady. Indeed, most were, if not ladies, then comfortably middle class with the demeanour and vowels that reflected expensive private education. British models were considered the best, and in great demand in Paris. Bronwen Pugh became Pierre Balmain's favourite. Jean Dawnay, who worked as a house model for Christian Dior for a season, was offered a contract with Jacques Fath and Carven within three days of arriving in France.

American models had little currency on the catwalks of Europe, although US photographers like Henry Clarke, Irving Penn and Avedon preferred to work with them for *Harper's Bazaar* and *Vogue*. They created their own stars. Avedon worked as much as possible with Suzy Parker, whose looks intrigued Chanel, even though she said that her neck was too long for success. Penn featured Lisa Fonssagrives, the woman he married, and Ann Saint-Marie was a favourite with Clarke. These partnerships altered the face of modelling, and paved the way for what was to

199

come in the 1980s. The modern concept of the model who jets into the fashion capitals of the world in order to do runway shows as an interruption – albeit an important one – in her normal work as a photographic model did not exist in the 1950s. The model's job then was 80 per cent showing clothes, 20 per cent being photographed. Even grand models were happy to be tied to a prestigious fashion house as a house model, something which would be unthinkable today. Modern fashion houses employ one or two house models who – true clothes-horses – stand for hours each day as clothes are tried on them and adjustments and alterations made. These women do not show the clothes to the public. High-profile superstars are employed for that. House models today are nuts-and-bolts members of the designer's team, with no more glamour than his assistants or heads of workrooms.

In the 1950s the great couturiers of Paris had their own stables of models, most of whom worked exclusively for them. Christian Dior's 'girls' – Sylvie, France, Lucky, Renée, Praline – became famous not for themselves, but for bringing something unique to the designer, which acted as inspiration. As he wrote in his autobiography, 'They alone can bring my clothes to life . . . the existence of a real affinity between a couturier and his mannequins is so vital.' House mannequins worked with the couturier every day. Embroiled in the daily creative battle, they understood the clothes which eventually emerged. They also showed his collection to private customers and to anyone sufficiently interested to obtain a ticket for his shows.

Most of the grand couturiers showed only couture to the press and private customers and, if they had a second, *jeune fille* range, it was confined to the house boutique. House models showed the clothes every afternoon to an audience of perhaps 25 to 50 women, often accompanied by their husbands or lovers and frequently with their *vendeuse* at their side. This is how a model like Jean Dawnay found employment for a whole season. Any photographic work that she and other models were able to do was undertaken out of business hours, in the evening or early morning. The real job was showing the clothes to a live audience.

The split between models who showed and those who posed was not to become a rift until the 1970s when, near the end of the decade, there was a huge demand in Europe for runway models who were black. Whereas earlier there had been a crossover in that runway models also did photographic work, black models – even of the stature of Billie Blair and Pat Cleveland, the first runway superstars – were not acceptable to any but specialist magazines, for either editorial or advertising pages. All magazine images until the mid-1980s reflected a Middle American look, which was blonde, blue-eyed and pale-skinned. Lauren Hutton netted a $500,000 contract with Revlon, and Cheryl Tiegs earned at least $300,000 a year in the late seventies. Both were over 30, but that was not important. Both were white, as were other top photographic models such as Margaux Hemingway and Candice Bergen, and that was what mattered. Black models were confined to the runway.

And they made it their own, bringing to Paris and Milan an unashamed sensuality and confidence as far from ladylike as anything could be. Phalanx after phalanx marched down the runways with military precision, jackbooting the old conventions underfoot, their raucous screams and overwhelming ebullience making white models look colourless and without character. They were the precursors of the 1980s supermodels – the big Americans who were so sassy, streetwise and healthy that the ladylike image projected by British and French models in the past was killed and buried for all time.

The silent salon through which a model glided in the Fifties, carrying a number or showing a dress that was christened with a fanciful name – Candy Kisses, Love in the Afternoon – over a loudspeaker as she entered was as far removed from Seventies ready-to-wear presentations as *Les Sylphides* is from rap. No music, no dazzling lights were allowed to distract. Like votaries at a solemn ceremony, the audience concentrated their attention on the clothes, which were expected to speak for themselves and be viewed as an entity. The whole concept of a 'show' was to come. When it did, it was the black models who made it a show to remember. And they made an even more fundamental contribution: after them, modelling was no longer the preserve of the middle classes. White girls like Twiggy and Jerry Hall and a host of lesser names poured through the breach made by black runway models, but their battleground was the photographer's studio much more than the designer's runway. The new models in either place were not interested in peddling an outmoded concept of ladylike class. They reflected the mood of the times and were in demand for their uniqueness and individuality. The model as personality was just around the corner.

She came into her own thanks to Andy Warhol. He made the top models into A-list people. The king of image and star-maker extraordinaire, he understood Vreeland's dictum that 'A model becomes what today is, and what today is is the inner force of fashion.' But he went further, seeing models as worthless in themselves but important as cultural icons, which underlined his belief that there is no distinction between quality and junk. But, even though he despised what models stood for, he gave them the profile that enabled them to be stars wherever they wished to go, from Studio 54 to late-night chat shows and beyond.

Although models in the 1990s are harder, more assured and more professional than their predecessors, it is only the projection that has changed. The job remains the same. The piratical board 'em and beat 'em sort of woman who made modelling super-newsworthy in the 1980s was selling herself to a public much more eager to buy into her world and lifestyle than to purchase the clothes. As the 1980s began to disintegrate and the emptiness of the

1990s became apparent, designers and manufacturers realised that models had a real role to play in the commercial equation of selling clothes to people who do not necessarily wish to buy. Image took over dress about a millennium ago, when choice was first permitted. It has been the point of fashion ever since. What makes the present decade different is the fact that the image projectors have become more important than the image they project. When Naomi fell, how many remember what she was wearing – apart from the infamous platform soles? We all know that Linda Evangelista makes in excess of $2 million a year. How many can recall one outfit, let alone its maker, that she has worn in the last five years? The effect is as if we had listened to an orchestra playing several pieces and then remembered only the name of the conductor, not the composers.

The fashion world is vulgar. Its *raison d'être* is making money. Costs and salaries, profits and loss, are bandied about as if they alone gave meaning to the fashion business. The man whose shows cost more than others is seen as a more successful designer. The man who breaks all records with his advertising budget is assumed to be cleverer than the others. And so the chase begins. Instead of asking *why* so much money has been spent, everybody else feels inferior until they're spending the same amount. That is how mega-models have become the richest class of working women in the world, excluding a few cinema superstars. When the first agency pushed up a model's fee and the designer, instead of saying, 'OK. That's her price, but not for me,' paid up and *told* everyone that he had, the hype had begun. Greedy models, haunted by the brevity of their moneymaking years, were happy to cooperate with grasping agencies. When Linda made her notorious remark about not getting out of bed for less than $10,000 a day, the fashion world, instead of condemning such vulgarity and quietly dropping her, found her even more desirable and fought to pay her more. The Nineties have seen the upward spiral checked but there is no guarantee that Eighties excesses will not return when money becomes less tight.

In the Eighties, building societies loaned twice as much money as they knew a house to be worth; car manufacturers added refinements costing hundreds to cars for which they upped the price by thousands; restaurateurs made up their prices on the back of a cigarette packet with no reference to cost of food or time of preparation and came up with bills for a dinner for two well in excess of £100. All did so, knowing that the prices would be met and that, after the shock, a certain pleasure could be found in paying so much. Thus, life in the Eighties became an adjunct to fashion which, in itself, perfectly fitted Wilde's remark on cynicism: a world where the price was important and the value rarely understood.

In the 1990s the price of clothes has faltered. We are less inclined to pay through the nose in order to be part of the dream. Paradoxically, the value and importance of models – although not their salaries – has rocketed to such an extent that a super-waif like Kate Moss can be catapulted into stardom at 19 on the whim of a designer and a photographer. This is the appalling thing that has happened to us all. Our parameters can be drawn by the likes of Calvin Klein and Steven Meisel so that we appear to enjoy our tastes being formed by such questionable gurus. Kate Moss, totally unexceptional in every way, has become a totem for our times. She will use Concorde as casually as she once used buses in her home town of Croydon. She will travel by private plane. She will come to know the most exclusive Caribbean islands, will swim in the most exotic pools, dine at the greatest tables, appear on – and possibly even host – chat shows, as Cindy Crawford does, and be paid $200,000 to write a novel as Naomi has, or, as in Claudia Schiffer's case, be asked to pen her autobiography at the age of 23. She will be on Christian-name terms with the whole world.

Mankind has always viewed beauty unrealistically. In the 1980s, certain designers and some magazine editors became excited by the ghostly unreality of pre-pubescence and its unmarked perfection. Fourteen-year-olds were made to look 20 and dressed in clothes created with women nearer 30 in mind. There is nothing exceptional in this. Fashion's love affair with youthful looks is not new: in the early Fifties, Christian Dior's model Tania was showing clothes aimed at women well over 30 in the salon of Lucien Lelong when she was only 16. Brooke Shields was 12 when, wearing men's clothes, she first posed for Bruce Weber. But the Eighties' obsession with child-women as models was rather more complicated because society had changed its attitudes. Photographers, art editors and designers projected the child model as a symbol of sexuality. Adults were encouraged to pant after her. Her fragile innocence was meant to be a turn-on. She was not made to look twice her age: it was her youth we were meant to lust after. Fortuitously and coincidentally, society at the same time became interested in child prostitution with a force and intensity not seen since Victorian times. The question is: did fashion initiate or merely reflect a trend? Either way, the modern model is clearly much more than a pretty face. In the last ten years she has become a conduit for attitudes and approaches unthought of in the era of Dior's Tania.

Curiously, many of these ambivalent pictures are the work of female photographers. Cindy Palamo and Corinne Day, for example, have been responsible for some of the most disquieting fashion pictures since Guy Bourdin. They present teenage girls as knowing, ready and aware of their power over men. But they have another quality. Their lenses almost drool over the unspoilt and unfulfilled expressions of these very young and immature models in a way which, were the photographers male, would excite angry feminist responses. There is an indefinable decadence in them. Shadows of an irregular and hidden world, with echoes of forbidden sexual experiences, seem to play over these perfect young features. But, somehow, feminists do not find such naked explorations of female sexuality a betrayal when the photographer is a woman.

The figures are not just fashionably thin, they are almost always anorexically so. Fashion apologists are ready to remove what fashion does from the common arena where questions of morality and manipulation must be answered. 'We propose,' they claim, in the time-honoured cop-out, 'but the public decides.' They forget that fashion's force is based on emulation, and what a designer or photographer proposes is tantamount to an edict for millions of young women who see their appearance as their major currency. Fashion magazines project images of perfection, and if those images demand stick-thinness then editors and photographers must take responsibility for the social consequences of their decisions.

For the first thirty years of this century, most fashion magazines used artists to illustrate fashion. The roll-call of great fashion artists is impressive, including names of men who captured the Zeitgeist in the drawings – often deceptively simple, even slapdash at first glance – they produced for *Vogue* and *Harper's Bazaar* in the 1920s and 1930s, for both covers and editorial pages. Benito, Iribe, Erté, Lepape – these were men honoured by editors and artists; men who found no inconsistency in using their considerable skills to illustrate something as transient as the current mode; men who saw fashion illustration in terms of page design; men whose choice of background detail, colour and decorative devices fixed a period for ever within the covers of the glossy magazines. Even when photography began to make inroads, the paranoia of couturiers, terrified of plagiarism, meant that photographers and cameras were distrusted in the couture world. As late as the 1950s, Christian Dior is reputed to have personally escorted to the door of his salon a woman whose elaborately trimmed hat hid a miniature camera, to banish her from his premises for ever. In those days, exclusivity was what drove fashion; now it is driven by publicity, and the photographer is king.

The making of a model is not a predetermined thing. There are many paths to the golden moment when her face appears on the cover of *Vogue*, or she steps on to the runway alone as the bride who traditionally ends a couturier's show. The first step can be taken while she is still literally a girl – some agencies have 11-year-olds on their books. Models have been 'spotted' in supermarkets, shopping malls, discos and school playgrounds by photographers, stylists, talent scouts from agencies and even other models. Kate Moss was noticed by Sarah Doukas, of Storm model agency, when she was standing with her father in an airline queue in New York. Claudia Mason was 14 when a talent scout noticed her in Tower Records, New York, and signed her for a shoot with Bruce Weber. How the first step is taken is unimportant. It is the subsequent moves that will decide how far a model can go in this highly competitive and overcrowded profession.

An international model agency will have hundreds of girls on its books who will never appear on a prestigious runway or smile out from the pages of a glossy magazine. According to the Ford agency figures, 30 per cent will be under 21 and 50 per cent between 21 and 30. Most of them will make a living and for many it will be a modest one, even though the working lifestyle seems glamorous. Often they will work in an exotic location – a Pacific island, a remote valley in Arizona – for a mass-market catalogue or on a promotional campaign for a downmarket product, and be paid handsomely. A sales pitch aimed at a high street chain often has a much more generous budget than one which will appear in limited upmarket outlets. Models command high fees only at the glamour end of the spectrum, when they have become glamorous themselves. Otherwise, to be linked with a prestigious name or appear in a top glossy is considered almost reward enough, and the money paid reflects that attitude.

In a sense, the attitude behind such thinking, which may seem manipulative and exploitative, is sound. For a model, one advertising page for Parfums Chanel is worth a thousand for a Boots own-brand campaign. A page in *Vogue* is worth a hundred in *Best*. Beginners in modelling are only as good as their last campaign and all subsequent work will almost certainly remain on that level. The vital necessity at the outset of a career is to be photographed by the right people, who do not have to be the photographic superstars but must be fashion insiders, known and trusted by magazine stylists, fashion directors and art editors. From their pictures, the model and her agency assemble her composite – the card which lists her statistics and contains two or three shots to convey her style and versatility. Only if the composite pleases will the model be seen in person by the photographer and stylist.

Being current is vital in a world where reputations are built on rumour and facts are taken less seriously than gossip. Models must be seen at the places where opinion-formers relax, be it the latest disco, the newest restaurant or the most 'in' party. Quite literally, you are only too often who you know, and you become known by who you are seen with. The few models who are going to become famous become famous very quickly. Photographers, hairdressers and make-up artists love to be seen with a new face, and everyone wishes to be the first to discover a new talent. Wise models are never surly at a photographic session, no matter how they may feel.

Making friends with fashionable hairdressers and make-up artists is fine, but the glittering prize is to work with, and become part of, the social entourage of an international photographer. It is not easy. Photographers have their pick of girls. But if Meisel likes a girl, so will everybody else, and *Vogue* and *Harpers* will be scrambling to be first to use her. She has become a hot property.

This is when the wise girl leaves things to her agency. A good booker is invaluable to a model and must have a close relationship with her. He does not need to be a friend, but he does require a level of intimacy and understanding. Money is obviously important but wise agencies take a long-term view and realise that making a career must come first. Anybody with a shrewd tongue can persuade a customer to use a model who is not right for an assignment, and many bookers offer discounted rates to make it happen, but it is a short-sighted policy. Good bookers nurture, knowing that, if they are right about a girl, the big money will come later.

In the final analysis, it is the photographers who are the real power brokers, wielding an influence greater even than that of the top designers. Modelling has changed out of all recognition since the days of Barbara Goalen, when the model was expected to provide her own accessories for a shoot, including shoes and jewellery, and do her own hair and make-up before stepping in front of the camera.

It was all so simple before the Sixties. Fashion editors and advertising managers required the photographers to create images of elegance. Models were to be photographed in a ladylike and sophisticated way. Even smoking a cigarette had to be done with panache. When in 1950 Norman Parkinson photographed Enid Boulting for English *Vogue* with a cigarette dangling from her mouth as she searched in her handbag for a light – a real piece of photographic vérité – the editor-in-chief of American *Vogue* cabled from New York: 'Smoking in *Vogue* so tough, so un-feminine.' An Irving Penn photograph of a model wearing Dior, her head held proudly back, smoking through a cigarette holder, was the accepted and acceptable glamorisation of such a banal act. The fact that such little details were important tells the tale of the times.

Many of the world's greatest photographers worked for *Vogue* and *Harper's Bazaar* in the first fifty years of this century, and some memorable images were produced. But the house style of these luxury magazines had a limiting effect on even those superlative talents. Flicking through the fashion pages from the 1920s to the

209

1950s begins as a marvellously exciting exercise but, as the years flip by, it becomes less stimulating until eventually you realise that what distinguishes these pictures is a deadening similarity, as if each photographer had been given precisely the same brief, regardless of the passing of years and changing social attitudes. And, in effect, he had. Obviously, a Beaton setting was different from a Horst; a Dahl-Wolfe lighting scheme was not the same as a Platt Lynes one; a Parkinson outdoor shot created a different atmosphere from one by Toni Frissell. But the images and mood were predictably alike, as were the models.

There were exceptions, people who broke out of the world dictated by their editors. But many of the most interesting received such short shrift that, original and exciting as their work was, it was almost as if, by making it so, they had put themselves beyond the pale. Already their names are almost forgotten. The fashion world still recalls Martin Munkacsi and the freedom of movement in his photographs, but who also remembers Herman Landshoff, who was following the same course? Even the trail-blazing technical experiments of Erwin Blumenfeld are now almost forgotten. Too much experimentation was frowned upon. Conformity was what brought rewards – until the arrival of Richard Avedon and Irving Penn.

But the leaders of the revolution were British. David Bailey, Terence Donovan and Brian Duffy, known as the 'Terrible Three', almost invented the Swinging Sixties and certainly created the images that gave it meaning far beyond London. Classless and styleless, as they were considered at the time, these photographers were no such thing. They were resolutely and unashamedly working class – in strong contrast to many of the top glossies' photographers of the past. Their style appeared as relaxed as a snap from a Brownie. They were cheeky and gutsy but, such was the power of the *Vogue* aura, the images were still safely middle class. Their interest was sex, not clothes, as Duffy's reference to his camera as a three-legged phallus makes clear. And it is sex that makes them even more important than Penn and Avedon, though artistically and technically far behind. Pre-Bailey, sex had been a question of allure, and sex appeal was manifested in and through the clothes. Post-Bailey, fashion photography kicked out allure, along with the tightly tailored suit and couture ballgown, and substituted street reality. The new approach required new models: Jean Shrimpton's homeliness superseded the cool sophistication of Lisa Fonssagrives; Penelope Tree's strangeness replaced the aloofness of Dovima; and Twiggy's stick-insect humour made the unattainable elegance of Dorian Leigh seem stiff, old-fashioned and almost ridiculous.

Personality had entered the realm of fashion photography. The new photographers, less inclined to be homosexual than the old guard, were not afraid to explore and parade their sexuality through their work. The shock of the unexpected put voltage into the least imaginative clothes. At the same time as 'reality' became the *sine qua non* of a good fashion picture, the photographers were taking the first strides towards the total unreality of their lives in the 1980s and 1990s. Following the idealisation of their work and existence in *Blow-Up*, they decided to ape the fantasy world the film projected. Suddenly they saw themselves as superstars and expected to be treated – and paid – like international pop idols.

Magazines and advertising swallowed the line, paid up and, more importantly, gave photographers unprecedented licence to create as they wished. Top photographers became members of the international super-rich elite, opinion-formers and taste-makers. They also became the mirror-holders for the middle classes, using their fashion spreads to reflect the unacceptable side of urban, free-for-all living. Sex, violence and drug-induced stasis became not the background to a picture but its content in the skilled work of Guy Boudin and Helmut Newton. Ambiguity gave way to straightforward portrayals of perversion.

Commercial magazines like American *Vogue* and *Harper's Bazaar* were locked in circulation battles and shied away from the new originality. The cutting edge of fashion photography was taken over by French *Vogue*, whose bold editorial stance in effect allowed Boudin and Newton to use the magazine's pages to play out their fantasies. For a remarkable few years they were afforded almost total artistic freedom, and they did not waste their opportunity. The images created for the editorial pages of French *Vogue* in the late Seventies were the strongest, most emotional fashion pictures ever produced. Boudin and Newton perfectly encapsulated the uncertainties of the decade.

Of course, their canvas was small and most people, including many in fashion, were unaware of their work at the time, but advertising brought it to a wider audience. In the mealy-mouthed 1990s, Oliviero Toscani's advertising campaign for Benetton has reaped much criticism, but the same shock tactics were used in the 1970s with much more style and sophistication in Guy Boudin's amazingly advanced advertising campaign for Charles Jourdain shoes. Eschewing the crude shock tactics beloved of Benetton, he produced brilliant pictures whilst losing none of the bite behind his campaign. In 1976 French *Vogue* ran an advertisement that featured a Boudin picture of a blood-soaked sidewalk with the white chalked outline of a female figure. A little way apart lie two white sandals. In its stark realism, it calls to mind police record photographs of the kind commercialised by the 1940s New York photographer, Weegee. It is a shocking picture, as it was meant to be, and puts Toscani's work on the level of a penny dreadful or a ghost train horror.

Powerful as Boudin and Newton's images were, they were not the only ones to disturb the bland pages of the glossy magazines. Some of the most unsettling images of the decade were produced by Deborah Turbeville, who took Diane Arbus's fascination with human alienation and made it part of fashion. Her women – and she usually used several in her pictures – are isolated and insulated from each other. They are withdrawn and self-involved: in the way that people deeply involved with fashion, Turbeville seems to be saying, are only interested in themselves. As fashion photographs they fail because the gulf between model and viewer is too wide to be bridged, but as fashion images they are superb.

As the 1970s merged into the 1980s, the hothouse unhealthiness of fashion photography gave way to the apparently more wholesome dream of uncomplicated rurality exploited by Bruce Weber. His images, strong and poetic, appealed because they were based on atavistic memories of rustic idylls long past. But, running beneath them, as strongly as lesbianism had in Seventies' pictures, was a powerful undercurrent of homo-eroticism. As the 1980s developed, the pin-up boy became the new icon for editorial and advertising imagery, and redefined the male runway model, all attitude and pulsating shaved chest.

Just as fashion is currently dormant, so photography is on hold. Peter Lindbergh, Steven Meisel, Ellen von Unsworth and Corinne Day are all – intentionally or not – rehoeing ground already thoroughly broken and raked clean. It is my view that nothing that is being done today has not already been done in the last thirty years. Maybe that is why fashion photographers have become such relentlessly social creatures, keeping their personal profile high because they suspect that so few of their images will be memorable.

Their love of 'stylish' living has become almost comical. Reports in the fashion press that Steven Meisel has added a cook to his entourage for fashion shoots might well be laughed off as a nonsense if the same thing were not said – and authenticated – of another photographer in the *Independent* in June 1993. Under the headline 'Putting on the Ritts', an article described a fashion shoot at Zuma Beach in California, Herb Ritts's favourite location, for which the photographer had assembled three assistants, a stylist and location manager, both with their assistants, and various others – ten in all. They included Herb's favourite cook, who prepared a meal of chicken legs, asparagus, green salad and tomato fusilli. All were there to help Ritts shoot a Sol beer advertisement and, perhaps, justify his fee of $140,000 for the day.

This kind of behaviour is matched by delusions of intellectual grandeur, and it looks as if the 1990s will see the pretentious utterances of designers echoed by those of photographers. A hint of things to come was provided by Oliviero Toscani when, justifying the United Colors of Benetton campaign which has featured a duck covered in oil, a dying AIDS victim, a newborn baby and a crowded refugee ship, he claimed, 'The advertising industry has corrupted society. It persuades people that they are respected for what they consume, that they are only worth what they possess . . . I want to make people think.' When a fashion photographer – or designer – sees that as part of his brief, fashion is in trouble.

12

London Pride

The fashion capital that has most clearly exposed the shifting sands on which the hype at the heart of the designer scam is based is London, a city unique in the way it pops in and out of fashion consciousness. Having almost wrested the lead from Paris in the 1960s, it lost it in the 1970s but came back briefly in the 1980s. London was never a city for high fashion innovation. Even Hartnell, Morton, Amies and their contemporaries from the 1930s to the 1950s, who produced many beautiful clothes, were not original. They closely followed the Paris line. British couturier Edward Molyneux, realising this, preferred working on the banks of the Seine to the banks of the Thames, although French houses such as Worth and Schiaparelli opened outlets in London for their British customers. London, nevertheless, has found a place on the sidelines of international fashion with its street-inspired looks that were hailed so uncritically in the late 1970s and early 1980s as a true fashion movement – at least, by homegrown journalists and promoters.

Such fashion has always contained the seeds of its downfall. No fashion succeeds commercially without wide appeal, as we have already seen. London's fashion ideas – and it has had many – achieve little that has any sense of permanency, because London fashion is fixated on youth, iconoclasm and individuality, which limit its appeal. Much of London fashion, beneath all the hype, has suffered from crippling immaturity and debilitating narcissism. Mark & Syrie, Body Map and Zwei might well have had an original eye and a strong desire to knock traditional fashion elitism off its pedestal, but making a permanent name takes thought, many years and something more subtle than shock tactics. London fashion designers wanted everything instantly. They were not prepared to put in the hours of learning either the craft or the business that characterised the success of one of London's genuinely successful, long-term talents, Jean Muir, whose work has a worldwide following. It is the difference between instant coffee and real. The former slakes the thirst of the moment, but only the latter satisfies.

Youth is carefree. Enthusiasm is its prerogative, caution its antithesis. Looking back on the Eighties and the collapse of London fashion, one cannot blame the designers. Young and unselfcritical, they were totally green. Older, wiser heads should have calmed them down, spruced them up and generally initiated them into the ways of the world. The tragedy of London fashion is that there were no such heads. A lot of people who should have known better were too busy shouting the odds like fairground barkers, in an attempt to convince us that these childish little talents were a force with some meaning outside the narrow confines of London art schools – their true spiritual home.

What was wrong with London style in the 1980s – and it has now spread throughout fashion – is that it had no ideals. Born out of class dissent, it did not wish to build, it wished to knock down. And, in true wrecker fashion, it had no discipline. The very first London show I attended, in a tent at Olympia, was an experience as traumatic as it was instructive. The name of the designer is not important. I recall it no more than I do the clothes. The lights dimmed, the audience was impatient. A slow hand-clap began. People started to whistle. We could barely see the runway for bodies milling around in front of us. Suddenly, a deranged bag-lady figure hurtled out on to the runway, swearing and waving her arms around. 'Sit down!' she screamed. 'Fucking sit down! Or the show won't begin.' I realised with a shock that this was not an entertainer sent out to warm us up before the show began, but the head of one of London's most respected and talented PR agencies whose work and enthusiasm had played a crucial role in setting up London fashion week.

I knew then that, in this city, there were no standards, no rigour, no discipline. I thought wistfully of Milan and Donatella Palazzi, the diplomat's wife who had worked with Armani on creating his coolly elegant lifestyle; the woman who, Italian journalists joked, had taught Versace how to use a knife and fork; the woman who, by a fractionally raised eyebrow, could quell any unseemly scene. My heart sank as I realised that Eighties London fashion would go the same sorry way as Sixties London fashion.

The 1960s were spoiled by a narcissistic lack of self-criticism. People did not say, 'I like it because it is good,' but, 'It's good because I like it'. 1980s London fashion was doomed to fail for the same reason.

In 1963 the Museum of Costume in Bath instituted the Dress of the Year scheme, to build up a collection of garments from key figures in the fashion world. For the first three years, the choice was made by the Fashion Writers' Association, a journalist group now long disbanded, but since 1966 the annual choice has been made by individual journalists who are fashion editors of prestigious newspapers like the *Times*, the *Telegraph* and the *Guardian*, or top magazines such as *Harpers & Queen*, *Vogue* and *Elle*. With such credentials the Bath Dress of the Year collection should be a roll-call of all that is great and good. Certainly many world-class names are represented: Karl Lagerfeld, Giorgio Armani, Ralph Lauren, Romeo Gigli and Jean Paul Gaultier are there. But what should have been an incomparable resource for future fashion journalists and historians is reduced by the plethora of second- and even third-rate designers who are represented for no conceivable reason than the fact that they are British.

In the thirty years since the Dress of the Year scheme was inititiated, Paris has produced designers of the quality of Claude Montana and Rei Kawakubo; Italy has given us Gianfranco Ferre and Dolce & Gabbana; from America have come Perry Ellis and Halston. None of these major figures is represented at Bath. Jean Muir, on the other hand, has been chosen twice. Hardy Amies, grand old man of English fashion, is missing, but Gina Fratini is present, as is John Bates. British fashion journalism is the most provincial in the world, more inward-looking than the French and more partisan than the Italians would dare to be.

It was not always so. We have produced fashion journalists who could bear comparison with the best of America or France although we have not, until recently, had editors of fashion magazines who could be mentioned in the same breath as Edna Woolman Chase or Diane Vreeland of American *Vogue*; Carmel Snow of *Harper's Bazaar* or Michel de Brunhoff of French *Vogue*. But in Prudence Glyn, mordantly witty and sharply critical; Alison Settle, wide-ranging and highly informed; Alison Adburgham, wearing vast learning with admirable lightness; and Ernestine Carter, surely the sharpest and most perceptive of all, British fashion journalism could field a clutch of writers equal, if not superior, to the great names of American fashion writing such as Bettina Ballard and Eugenia Sheppard, who are still honoured today. Why were their like not heard in the Eighties, the fashion decade?

One of the most pernicious developments in British society during that time was the rise of the colour supplement. No longer content with reporting the news, papers turned to pushing culture and lifestyle – how the rich live; the ten most desirable invitations in London, the ten best country-house loos in Scotland. Journalists were sent out by frantic editors to 'discover' new talent. Actors, painters, writers and, of course, designers, had to be garnered and exposed as quickly as possible. If no one else had covered them first, then they *had* to be good.

At the outset of the decade 'way-out' talent essentially was a manifestation of working-class alienation. But it was not allowed to monopolise the high ground for long: it was annexed by the middle classes, who immediately pasteurised it and tried to make it commercial. Guerrilla-warfare attempts to show alienation from a society arguably the most bourgeois in the world gave vigour to even the most self-indulgent exercises in street fashion at the beginning of the decade. By the end of the 1980s, what creativity was left was vested in upper-middle-class girls whose friends – and Daddy's bank – could keep them going.

Fashion is not central to our culture. Class is. Even in the Eighties, when a fashion society seemed to shine briefly in London, it still lagged a long way behind the glitter, gloss and sheer chutzpah of its New York equivalent. A glance at gossip columns and society pages shows the difference immediately. Look at Nigel Dempster in the *Daily Mail* and you see chronicles not of the fashionable but the well-born; read Jennifer's Diary in *Harpers & Queen* and you are invited to swallow uncritical listings of 'persons present'; flick through *Tatler* and, apart from a brief flowering of schoolgirl iconoclasm under the editorship of Tina Brown, you find nothing that for verve, wit and 'right-on' precision can hold a candle to Suzy in *Women's Wear Daily* – a column which does everything that the British society pages fail to achieve. Beneath Suzy's glittering words is the prod of the Devil's pitchfork which skewers pomposity and punctures self-importance.

Suzy has been around a long time, though even she cannot match the long-running stint of Jennifer – Betty Kenwood – in *Harpers & Queen*. But time and endless partying have done nothing to blunt her bite. That is why people with no interest in fashion read her column; why people have *WWD* shipped halfway round the world for their daily fix; why people would maim in order to be featured by her. Even though she might make fun of them, if they are mentioned, they are 'in'.

Why does London not have an Eleanor Lambert – and if it did, would she be the daughter of a circus worker from Crawfordsville, Indiana, or the daughter of a belted earl closely related to the monarch? The answer is inherent in the question. Eleanor Lambert has been the ringmaster of American fashion and fashionable society since 1943 when she inaugurated the Coty American Fashion Critics' Awards, which were soon to become the Oscars of the fashion business. Shortly after, she took over from the French their ailing and almost moribund Best-Dressed List and made it of compulsive interest to all in fashionable American society. From it sprang the In-Out lists of fashion that have become a staple of journalism in this country as well as America. But, even though it was rejected by those who felt the only criterion for inclusion was extreme wealth, the Best-Dressed List gave fashion journalism – and, of course, fashion itself – a high-profile credibility in America that it has never attained in Britain.

The rise and fall of Arabella Pollen brings together elements of almost everything that was good and bad about London fashion in the 1980s: talent, initiative and enterprise on one hand; chauvinism, unreality and indulgence on the other.

Pollen ran her own company, which had a turnover of £1.2 million in 1990. On paper, she was one of London's best bets: sporadically dressmaker to the Princess of Wales; daughter of a former head of Sotheby's in the US; member of the chattering classes; married to a wealthy and well-born Italian; socially impeccable and able to look quite good in her own well-bred clothes. In 1990 Courtaulds Textiles bought into her company. Chief executive Martin Taylor explained that Courtaulds' involvement would mean that 'She won't constantly be looking over her shoulder – when the economy improves, she'll still be around.' Three years later, in May 1993, the arrangement was discontinued.

Miss Pollen was part of a fashion phenomenon peculiar to London: the dressmaker writ large. There is a surprising number of them. Many of these cottage couturiers have quite good, if old-fashioned, taste; some have rudimentary design skills; few have any business knowledge or practical experience of production; but all have a pile of Fifties' *Vogues* – and friends. Not just friends and not always friends in really high places, but friends of sufficient number and grandeur to dine at the coveted SW6 tables where future customers for pretty but undemanding frocks, high on frills and low on ideas, can be found.

'I think it stupid to be governed by fashion,' Arabella Pollen said in an interview. 'It's relatively unimportant and certainly should never be taken seriously.' If such a remark were made by a theatre director or a conductor, there would be an outcry. People would ask, with perfect justification, 'All right, if you don't think drama or music should be taken seriously, why are you taking the money?'

When Courtaulds and Pollen parted, there was an outcry. The fashion press and the trade had no doubt about who was to blame. Yet another example of British talent being let down by unimaginative, uninspired and unreliable provincial businessmen, they whined. This theme song of British fashion was heard repeatedly during the 1980s as each overindulged or under-talented designer went bust.

The problem is not so much British as a London one. Most of the PRs and press who rail against the shortcomings of industrial backing haven't the slightest interest in provincial fashion designers unless they are prepared to make themselves available in London. Ask any of Scotland's young designers how easy it is to interest a London-based PR in their work; talk to a provincial manufacturer about the difficulty of wheedling a London journalist into a trip to a factory, and the extent of the problem is apparent. British fashion must be London fashion, or it is simply forgotten.

There is nothing unique in the situation. French fashion is Paris based, American fashion is largely a New York monopoly. In both cases, factories throughout the country – and, indeed, abroad – are served by the designers and, in turn, service their needs. London is different only because it does not have a network of provincial clothing manufacturers working to the demands of a core of top-rate designers. Most of the clothing factories that survive are working for huge chains like Marks & Spencer and C&A, or upmarket firms like Aquascutum or Jaeger. And why should they not? By doing so, they are guaranteed volume; subject to an insistence on quality, which keeps workmanship to a high level; and they are working with professional people – designers or accountants – who are practical, reliable and cost conscious. The time has surely come to stop blaming industry for not putting shareholders' money and employees' jobs at risk by refusing to back British dress designers. We must start looking elsewhere for our villains. We could do worse than start with the designers themselves. Put bluntly, they are not good enough for the big league. Only the best survive at that level.

Arabella Pollen's rise and fall have been comparatively swift. More enduring talent often requires much longer in order to establish itself in London. Think of Vivienne Westwood. It has taken over twenty years for her to find acceptance. That it has happened at all to someone born to be an outsider, an irritant to the fashion hierarchy, is ridiculous. That *she* has accepted this acceptance could be seen as a tragic end to a career previously dedicated to operating beyond the limits of social approval.

Vivienne Westwood has gone soft. She has allowed herself to be clasped to the bosom of the fashion Establishment as a lovable old eccentric, someone of whom fashion should be proud, someone as quintessentially British as a golden retriever. Neglected and laughed at for years, she subversively stood her ground and became the thing that all designers long to be: a cultural force. She has dwindled, it seems to me, into just another maker of clothes specialising in crazy, uncommercial ideas of the sort that can be found in the sketchpad of any first-year fashion student. In the Seventies, almost single-handed, Vivienne Westwood invented punk dressing as fashion. She was a crucial catalyst for all those who railed against a corrupt and uncaring society. In the Nineties it is possible to imagine her accepting the title of Baroness Westwood of World's End.

Fig leaves, mini-crinis and royal crowns chart her fall from grace. There are even signs that she has become commercially viable after years of near insolvency. Having twice accepted that dubious accolade of small-town respectability, the British Fashion Council's Designer of the Year award, Westwood's aspirations are now towards intellectuality. She talks much of philosophy and literature, of Rousseau, Bertrand Russell and Huxley. She sees herself as a second Madame Récamier, with a salon of the intellectually and artistically brilliant. This is all harmless enough, but where Westwood shows some of her old shrewdness is in the canny way she has pre-empted history's criticism of her dress-making skills by suggesting that not only her fashion philosophy but also her methods are in direct line of descent from the great couturiers of the past, such as Christian Dior.

Westwood is now being hyped as proof positive of the legendary supremacy of English fashion, as if one outsider brought into the fold makes a movement. But there are other, equally persistent, myths that bolster the belief that London could one day become a fashion powerhouse. One of the most constant is the claim that English colleges of fashion are superior to all others. It is true that fashion graduates from Britain are found in quite large numbers abroad, working as 'design assistants' to many of the top Italian and French designers. As toilers in the field, they are indeed welcome. They can be paid badly, no responsibility for their welfare in sickness or unemployment need be taken and they can be sacked with impunity. English art school graduates working in fashion houses in Europe have about the same status as their direct counterparts: the immigrant workers from Turkey, North Africa and the Eastern bloc who are employed in Germany, France and many other EC countries as sweated labour. To assess the real value put on English designers abroad it is only necessary to recall that, of the thousands who went out to conquer the world, only Alan Cleaver and Keith Varty have ever been allowed to stand in the sun – as named designers for the Italian firm, Byblos.

At least the young art school graduates abroad are learning their trade in the traditional and soundest way – at the feet of a maestro. Four weeks spent in planning a collection with Gianfranco Ferre; four days of fittings with Mariuccia Mandelli of Krizia; four hours watching Armani accessorising his clothes for a show are worth four years hanging around an art school.

As the European recession deepens, there is less need for the numbers of graduates we produce. Better by far to reduce drastically the number of colleges and use the money to support students working at the coalface in British industry and with foreign firms. Think how many fashion magazines could be bought for them with the money saved on tutors' salaries alone, quite apart from the enhanced prospects of work that a reduction in the number of graduates would bring. After all, as Karl Lagerfeld has said of his profession, 'You don't have to study that hard or go to boring schools. It's not that difficult.'

Recession weeds out the weakest in business as ruthlessly as drought does in nature. Those who survive do so stronger and more likely to withstand the next financial slump. Maybe the London fashion world will look back at the 1990s with gratitude, for cutting out so much dead wood.

Even if it does, it seems likely that London fashion is destined to sleep for another twenty years. Even successful designers like Muir and Jasper Conran might not have the financial resources to weather another five years of recession. When the going gets tough, the tough spend money. And this is why British fashion is so disadvantaged. There is no cash in the pot. No one in this country has the funds for a move as bold as Ralph Lauren's in capturing the college market with his new Double RL casual range. In autumn 1993 he hit the road with an 18-wheeler, 65-foot-long mobile showroom and shop – emblazoned with wild stallions on one side and images of Lauren clothes on the other – to tour campuses across the States, complete with nine staff and back-up truck full of merchandise in order to lasso the next generation of Ralph Lauren aficionados almost as part of their college education.

The British Fashion Council, trying to keep the doomed and leaking ship of British fashion afloat, must look with despair at Paris, and its 7-million-franc permanent venue for the Paris fashion shows, with four halls capable of seating almost 4,000 people at any one time. It is all a question of money.

As it is for us, the customers. Over the last decade, in my opinion, we have been abused and misled by a frequently ruthless and immoral industry determined to scam us into believing that high fashion clothing is a birthright, a proof of worth, an adjunct of character, even an indication of social desirability. That industry is now running scared at what it fears might prove a permanent shift in consumer aspirations and spending. It is terrified in case luxury ready-to-wear never becomes profitable again. It stares bleakly at a future dominated by the likes of Benetton and The Gap.

Whether such fears will be realised only time can tell. The pattern of acquisition promulgated throughout the 1980s – the 'I want, I need, I will have' formulaic response to cunning advertising and media manipulation – might return, but it does not have to do so. It is up to us.

I wrote this book because I believe that fashion plays an important role in all of our lives. I believe that beautiful clothes – like all good design – enhance the soul beyond considerations of mere function. It is because I love fashion and believe in the

225

ultimate value of what the fashion world produces that I have attempted to expose the worthlessness of the designer scam. Having done so, I hope that 'caveat emptor' will not be the rallying cry for fashion consumers in the twenty-first century.

Index

227